Jesus Will Set The Captives Free

Evangelist Joan Pearce

HCP BOOK
PUBLISHING
www.hcpbookpublishing.com

Cover design by Jim & Robin Art.

All Scriptures, unless otherwise stated, are taken from the Holy
Bible, New King James Version Copyright © 1982 by Thomas
Nelson, Inc. Used by permission. All rights reserved. Bible used
was the Holy Bible NKJV, Nashville: Thomas Nelson, 1994.

ISBN: 9781689644396 (paperback)

First Edition: January 2020

Printed in the United States of America

Dedication

I would like to thank my Lord and Savior Jesus Christ for saving my soul and writing my name in the Lamb's Book of Life.

I want to thank the Lord Almighty for leading and guiding me to write this book according to His will. To God be the glory forever! Amen.

Without the leading of the Holy Spirit, this book would not have been written and published. For it is written, "Not by might nor by power, but by My Spirit," says the Lord of hosts. (Zechariah 4:6)

A personal thanks to my beloved husband, Marty, and to my children: Alan, Rob, and Carrie for their continued encouragement.

Thank you to Jim & Robin Art for their labor of love on the cover design of this book.

I want to thank God for bringing me His servant, Cleveland O. McLeish, CEO of HCP Book Publishing, who worked so many hours on this book. I thank God for the gift of wisdom He placed in him.

I pray this book will inspire you who read it and bring you into a place of fulfillment and be an answer to your prayers.

There are so many others God has brought to me to be a blessing. There isn't enough paper in this book to thank them all by name. Sincere thanks to each one of you.

May God richly bless you.

Joan Pearce

Table of Contents

Introduction

I n today's world, there are many people suffering from demonic possession or oppression. By simply watching the news, visiting a local doctor's office or hospital or taking a walk down the street, we see that there are many people who are suffering in one way or another. The most common causes for their suffering are demons.

There are evil spirits loose in our world today. We call them demons, bad spirits, devils, and the name of their leader is Satan, who was once a beautiful angel, but is now a fallen entity. Satan and his demons are causing havoc on our world. Their sole purpose is to steal, kill and destroy, but Jesus came to give life and life more abundantly. Through the death, burial and resurrection of Jesus, normal people who are called Believers in Christ or Christians have been given power and authority over the evil demons. The Bible says there is a power you can receive called the infilling of the Holy Spirit, yet, a lot of Christians are not even aware of this power or they are too afraid to step out in faith and carry out the mandate given to us by Jesus to go and set the captives free.

I have written this book not only to open your eyes to the truth of the presence of evil in our world, but also to the reality that you have the power to set the captives free. God gave you that power, and He expects you to use it to set at liberty those who are lost and in darkness so they can come to know Jesus as Lord and Saviour.

Demons are blocking a lot of people from knowing God because they blind them to the truth, and oppress them with sicknesses, trauma and calamities that keep them distracted from pursuing the truth.

This book seeks to answer the questions you may have about the origin and purpose of Satan and his demons. Most importantly, you will know who you are in Christ, what you carry, and the power and authority you have to set the captives free through the cross and blood of Jesus Christ.

Chapter 1
The Thief Comes To Steal, Kill & Destroy

The Lord Jesus came to earth to set us free, to break the chains of the fall of Adam and Eve and give us liberty. God wants us to be free in everything we do and say. The questions a lot of people ask are, "Who is Satan? Where did he come from? Why is he harassing everybody?" You need to know the answers to these questions because God has a special plan for your life.

> **For I know the thoughts that I think toward you, says the Lord, thoughts of peace and not of evil, to give you a future and a hope. (Jeremiah 29:11).**

God wants to bless and prosper you and He has great plans for your life. Satan hates God's creation, and Satan wants to make sure you don't fulfill God's plan for your life.

The thief does not come except to steal, and to kill, and to destroy. I have come that they may have life, and that they may have it more abundantly. (John 10:10).

Satan comes to steal, kill, and destroy. There is a war going on and we are a part of this war. This war is between two kingdoms: the kingdom of Jesus and the kingdom of Satan.

He has delivered us from the power of darkness and conveyed us into the kingdom of the Son of His love. (Colossians 1:13).

God delivered us out of the kingdom of darkness and into the kingdom of Jesus by the Cross of Calvary when Jesus paid the price to redeem us back to what we would have been in the very beginning. Man was created perfect, but fell to sin because of Satan, who is a deceiver. He is good at deceiving and has been deceiving people from the very beginning. He has not changed because he is a liar and the father of lies.

Now the serpent was more cunning than any beast of the field which the Lord God had made. And he said to the woman, "Has God indeed said, 'You shall not eat of every tree of

the garden'?" And the woman said to the serpent, "We may eat the fruit of the trees of the garden; but of the fruit of the tree which is in the midst of the garden, God has said, 'You shall not eat it, nor shall you touch it, lest you die.'" Then the serpent said to the woman, "You will not surely die. For God knows that in the day you eat of it your eyes will be opened, and you will be like God, knowing good and evil." So when the woman saw that the tree was good for food, that it was pleasant to the eyes, and a tree desirable to make one wise, she took of its fruit and ate. She also gave to her husband with her, and he ate. Then the eyes of both of them were opened, and they knew that they were naked; and they sewed fig leaves together and made themselves coverings. And they heard the sound of the Lord God walking in the garden in the cool of the day, and Adam and his wife hid themselves from the presence of the Lord God among the trees of the garden. Then the Lord God called to Adam and said to him, "Where are you?" So he said, "I heard Your voice in the garden, and I was afraid because I was naked; and I hid myself." And He said,

13

"Who told you that you were naked? Have you eaten from the tree of which I commanded you that you should not eat?" (Genesis 3:1-11).

How does Satan get into our heads? How does Satan come and torment us? It all starts in the mind. If we don't renew our minds and have our minds centered on the Word of God; if we don't spend time meditating on the Word of God, and keeping our minds on Jesus, the devil will come and put his own thoughts there. These thoughts are all lies because they come from the father of lies and we should not believe them.

So, let's talk about who Satan is and where he came from.

How you are fallen from heaven, O Lucifer, son of the morning! How you are cut down to the ground, You who weakened the nations! (Isaiah 14:12).

Satan has been around longer than we can count. What has he done over the last thousands of years? He weakens nations by strife, envy, etc. He knows how to turn people against each other and uses deception to weaken the nations. So, he is a destroyer of nations.

For you have said in your heart: 'I will ascend into heaven, I will exalt my throne above the stars of God; I will also sit on the mount of the congregation on the farthest sides of the north; I will ascend above the heights of the clouds, I will be like the Most High.' Yet you shall be brought down to Sheol, to the lowest depths of the Pit. (Isaiah 14:13-15).

God is saying to Satan, "You think you're going to be something but you're not."

Those who see you will gaze at you, and consider you, saying: 'Is this the man who made the earth tremble, who shook kingdoms, who made the world as a wilderness and destroyed its cities, who did not open the house of his prisoners?' (Isaiah 14:16-17).

When this is all over and we are in heaven looking over at Satan, we are going to look at him and say, "Is this what did this to the whole world, to a whole planet? How could this be?" Satan is strong, but we are stronger. If we lack knowledge and we don't know how to recognize the influence of Satan and the demon forces, we will think they are stronger than us. That is why God gave us the gifts of the Holy Spirit (See Corinthians 12). He gave us a gift of discerning of spirits so when we get around people, we can discern what is going on inside of them. When we operate in the gifts of the Spirit, it doesn't take long to know what kind of person we are dealing with, whether they are trying to manipulate us or charming us like a snake charmer. The gifts allow us to recognize the forces of the enemy because we are not to be caught offguard. We need to be wise and be prayed up and know and be able to discern what is going on.

We also have power because of Jesus to tell devils to leave. According to Scripture, we can put the devils under our feet and they will be like ashes under our feet. We can turn devils into powder because we have the power.

> But to you who fear My name the Sun of Righteousness shall arise with healing in His wings; and you shall go out and grow fat like stall-fed calves. You shall trample the wicked, for they shall be ashes under the soles of your feet on the day that I do this," says the Lord of hosts. (Malachi 4:2-3).

"How you are fallen from heaven, o Lucifer, son of the morning! How you are cut down to the ground, you who weakened the nations! For you have said in your heart: 'I will ascend into heaven, I will exalt my throne above the stars of God; I will also sit on the mount of the congregation on the farthest sides of the north; I will ascend above the heights of the clouds, I will be like the Most High.' Yet you shall be brought down to Sheol, to the lowest depths of the Pit. Those who see you will gaze at you, and consider you, saying: 'Is this the man who made the earth tremble, who shook kingdoms, who made the world as a wilderness and destroyed its cities, who did not open the house of his prisoners?' All the kings of the nations, all of them, sleep in glory, everyone in his own house; but you are cast out of your grave like an abominable branch, like the garment of those who are slain, thrust through with a sword, who go down to the stones of the pit, like a corpse trodden underfoot. You will not be joined with them in burial, because you have destroyed your land and slain your people.

17

**The brood of evildoers shall never be named."
(Isaiah 14:12-20).**

Lucifer wants to exalt himself and he wants to be God because he said, "I will exalt myself." There are demonic fallen angels because Lucifer was cast out of heaven along with one third of the angels who joined him in his rebellion. Can you imagine what kind of influence Lucifer must have had to convince angels that are already in heaven with God Almighty, to rebel? He is a chief deceiver.

> **And war broke out in heaven: Michael and his angels fought with the dragon; and the dragon and his angels fought, but they did not prevail, nor was a place found for [b]them in heaven any longer. So the great dragon was cast out, that serpent of old, called the Devil and Satan, who deceives the whole world; he was cast to the earth, and his angels were cast out with him. (Revelation 12:7-9).**

I believe there are fallen angels who possess people. Hitler, for example, and Napoleon had demons that operated through them to do what they did. It is said that when Hitler died, all of a sudden his followers came to their senses. Even those who had killed Jews, all of a sudden, when they knew Hitler was dead, it was like something came off them because he had a demonic spirit in that realm that was controlling people. There are demonic powers that can control an entire nation.

Lucifer wants to control people. He wants to get inside people because he is building an army. There are different ranks of demonic forces, just like God has different ranks of angels. It can be likened to a military force preparing for battle. It is a battle between good and evil. Satan is trying to get as many people as he can to take them to hell with him.

Another question people ask is: "If God is God, why did He make Lucifer?"

God did not create Lucifer as a demon. Lucifer was one of the highest-ranking angels; a cherubim angel in the throne room of God. It is amazing how those who are the closest to us can be the ones who stab us in the back. I am sure God was aware of what Lucifer was up to and what he was going to do. The Bible says:

> **All who dwell on the earth will worship him, whose names have not been written in the Book of Life of the Lamb slain from the foundation of the world. (Revelation 13:8).**

The next day John saw Jesus coming toward him, and said, "Behold! The Lamb of God who takes away the sin of the world!" (John 1:29).

And they overcame him by the blood of the Lamb and by the word of their testimony, and they did not love their lives to the death. Therefore rejoice, O heavens, and you who dwell in them! Woe to the inhabitants of the earth and the sea! For the devil has come down to you, having great wrath, because he knows that he has a short time. (Revelation 12:11-12).

And they sang a new song, saying: "You are worthy to take the scroll, and to open its seals; for You were slain, and have redeemed us to God by Your blood out of every tribe and tongue and people and nation, and have made us kings and priests to our God; and we shall reign on the earth." Then I looked, and I heard the voice of many angels around the throne, the living creatures, and the elders; and the number of them was ten thousand times ten thousand, and thousands of thousands, saying with a loud voice: "Worthy is the Lamb who was slain to receive power and riches and wisdom, and strength and honor and glory and blessing!" (Revelation 5:9-12).

The Father, Son, and Holy Spirit already knew that this plan was going to unfold this way and they already had the answer to the problem. The answer is Jesus Christ and Him crucified. Jesus is the mediator between man and God, and they already had a plan. They saw what Lucifer was going to do. They didn't get caught off guard. In the same way, Jesus knew Judas was going to betray him. He wasn't caught off guard. He knew what Lucifer was going to do.

We need to be aware of the devil's devices. He was an angel; a very beautiful angel.

Son of man, take up a lamentation for the king of Tyre, and say to him, 'Thus says the Lord God: "You were the seal of perfection, full of wisdom and perfect in beauty. You were in Eden, the garden of God; every precious stone was your covering: the sardius, topaz, and diamond, beryl, onyx, and jasper, sapphire, turquoise, and emerald with gold. The workmanship of your timbrels and

21

pipes was prepared for you on the day you were created."' (Ezekiel 28:12-13).

Satan was already in Eden, in the garden of God. That is why he was able to tempt Adam and Eve. Every precious stone was his covering. He was beautiful to look at. Satan was created by God, not to be evil but iniquity was found in him. He was lifted up in pride.

Pride is the number one killer of many ministries. Some ministries that moved mightily in the supernatural have hit the dust. They were lifted up in pride because they started seeing miracles happening through their hands. They saw people come out of wheelchairs, and many wonderful miracles and it was not even them doing it. It was God working through them as a vessel. We are privileged and honored to be used of God, but when we start thinking it is us, then pride sets in. Pride always comes before a fall. So, we must remember that Lucifer, this beautiful cherubim angel, was in charge of music.

Today, we see Satan using music to destroy people here on earth. That is what he did in heaven. His department was in charge of music and it must have been beautiful music. So now, the music down here on earth gets distorted and I am sure Satan has gone to many musicians, movie stars and business people and made them a deal. He will promise you fame for worship. He tried to make a deal with Jesus. Jesus was on a 40-day fast and Satan tried to make a deal with Jesus.

> **And he said to Him, "All these things I will give You if You will fall down and worship me." (Matthew 4:9).**

Jesus said to the devil, ""**Away with you, Satan! For it is written, 'You shall worship the Lord your God, and Him only you shall serve.'" (Matthew 4:10).** There are some people who sell their souls for fame, but when they are in hell, the reality is going to hit them. They are going to realize that they sold out too cheaply.

Satan will make a deal, then make you famous, and then he will get you hooked on drugs, etc. If fame, money and beauty was all we needed in life, why are so many people who fall into this category committing suicide? Because the devil is working overtime in the minds of people.

> **You were the anointed cherub who covers; I established you; you were on the holy mountain of God; You walked back and forth in the midst of fiery stones. You were perfect in your ways from the day you were created,**

till iniquity was found in you. (Ezekiel 28:14-15).

Satan was created perfect. Iniquity came in and started messing him up. He was filled with pride; lifted up in sin and, therefore, he wants to bring people with him down into the pit. In the book of Revelation, we read about the war that happened in heaven. Michael and the angels fought against the dragon and the demon and they were cast out to earth. When Adam and Eve fell into sin, all of creation went into bondage. Jesus had to come and set us free, and that is what God wants to do.

For as in Adam all die, even so in Christ all shall be made alive. But each one in his own order: Christ the firstfruits, afterward those who are Christ's at His coming. Then comes the end, when He delivers the kingdom to God the Father, when He puts an end to all rule and all authority and power. For He must reign till He has put all enemies under His feet. The last enemy that will be destroyed is death. For "He has put all things under His feet." But when He says "all things are put under Him," it is evident that He who put all things under Him is excepted. Now when all

24

things are made subject to Him, then the Son Himself will also be subject to Him who put all things under Him, that God may be all in all. Otherwise, what will they do who are baptized for the dead, if the dead do not rise at all? Why then are they baptized for the dead? And why do we stand in jeopardy every hour? I affirm, by the boasting in you which I have in Christ Jesus our Lord, I die daily. If, in the manner of men, I have fought with beasts at Ephesus, what advantage is it to me? If the dead do not rise, "Let us eat and drink, for tomorrow we die!" Do not be deceived: "Evil company corrupts good habits." Awake to righteousness, and do not sin; for some do not have the knowledge of God. I speak this to your shame. But someone will say, "How are the dead raised up? And with what body do they come?" Foolish one, what you sow is not made alive unless it dies. And what you sow, you do not sow that body that shall be, but mere grain—perhaps wheat or some other grain. But God gives it a body as He pleases, and to each seed its own body. All flesh is not the same flesh, but there is one kind of flesh of men, another flesh of animals, another of fish, and another of birds. There are also celestial bodies and terrestrial bodies; but the glory of the celestial is one, and the glory of the terrestrial is another. There is one glory of the sun, another glory of the moon, and another glory of the stars; for one star differs from another star in glory. So also is the resurrection of the dead. The body is sown in corruption, it is raised in incorruption. It is sown in dishonor, it is raised in glory. It is sown in weakness, it is raised in power. It is sown a natural body, it is raised a spiritual body. There is a natural body, and there is a spiritual body. And so it is written, "The first man Adam became a living being." The last Adam became a life-giving spirit. (1 Corinthians 15:22-45).

God wants us to have victory over sin.

Chapter 2
Jesus Came That We Might Have Life

And my speech and my preaching were not with persuasive words of human wisdom, but in demonstration of the Spirit and of power, that your faith should not be in the wisdom of men but in the power of God. However, we speak wisdom among those who are mature, yet not the wisdom of this age, nor of the rulers of this age, who are coming to nothing. But we speak the wisdom of God in a mystery, the hidden wisdom which God ordained before the ages for our glory, which none of the rulers of this age knew; for had they known, they would not have crucified the Lord of glory. (1 Corinthians 2:4-8).

If Satan knew what was going to happen when Jesus was crucified, he would have left Jesus alone. He is a liar, but he doesn't know everything. He knows how to set traps for people because he has been doing it for centuries. He will get you depressed, then get you on drugs causing your life to spiral out of control. He will convince you that what you are doing is okay, then condemn you after you do it. The Bible refers to him as the "accuser of the brethren." He entices people. That is how he works. I believe people who commit abortions are prey to demonic spirits. It is only a devil that can convince someone to get rid of a baby.

The Spirit Of Murder

I want to share a story about how Satan works. We were in Alaska and we were out witnessing and talking to people about the Lord. I gave a particular lady a flier, and said to her, "If you ever need to call somebody to know more about Jesus, call me."

When we were back at the hotel, I was in my hotel room praying. I was praying for that lady that she would get saved because I knew she wasn't saved. She called. It is amazing how we can be praying and God immediately answers our heart's desire. I was praying for her soul and she called.

I called the pastor of the church we were visiting. I said to him, "We need to go see this lady but she doesn't know we are ministers. It's best if we don't tell her we're ministers."

We went to her house and as we settled in her living room, I said to her, "So what can we do for you? What's the problem?"

She said, "When you were at my house the other day, you shared that Jesus was the answer and I really need help. I need desperate help! I don't know what's going on with me. I think I'm losing my mind."

I said, "Well, tell me what's going on."

She said, "I hear a voice in my head. I have a brand-new baby. Shh, come I'll show you." So, we tiptoed across the room and she opened the door to the bedroom. We looked in and there was a beautiful baby, maybe eight months old, in a crib, sound asleep. She shut the door and we went back to the living room and sat down.

"So what's the problem? You've got a beautiful baby." I said.

She said, "I hear voices all the time."

I said, "What kind of voices?"

She said, "The voice says I should kill my baby. I'm so scared! The other day, I actually had my hands around its throat, and I was choking my baby. And then all of a sudden I came out of it and said 'What am I doing? I don't want to kill my baby!'"

She said the voice had been telling her repeatedly that her life was not going to be the same; that she would be tied down. She was not married and could not raise a baby. She would need to find an extra job.

I said to her, "That's a spirit."

That lady was being tormented and needed deliverance.

I remember a couple years ago there was a shooting in a bank in Florida. A man went into the bank and just started shooting people. When they captured him, he did not kill himself and he did not want any money. He was not in the bank to get any money. He just went in there to kill. There was no other motive. One of the policemen on the scene asked him, "Why did you do it?"

The man said, "I don't know. A voice has been telling me, 'Kill. Kill as many people as you can.'"

People who don't have Christ and are not renewed in their mind have no hope so they give up easily. The suicide rate is high because people lose hope and then a demon spirit attaches to them. Drinking and drugs is one way demons use to possess people.

The Bible says if the spirits of this age knew what they were doing when they were crucifying Jesus, they would have never crucified the Lord of glory because He won the victory through His death. When Jesus died on the cross, the devils probably had a party. They thought He was dead. But three days later, Jesus showed up and said, "Satan, there was a battle and I fought fair. Adam lost it, I got it back. Give me the keys to the kingdom and to the power of the kingdom of God." Whoever accepts Jesus Christ into their heart has the keys to the kingdom.

> **And I will give you the keys of the kingdom of heaven, and whatever you bind on earth will be bound in heaven, and whatever you loose on earth will be loosed in heaven. (Matthew 16:19).**

So we have power. God has given us the power to set the captives free. We don't have to sit around and watch our friends on drugs or being oppressed by demons and not do anything about it. We need to step out. Jesus is saying to us, "You have the power to set the captives free. You have the power to tell the demonic spirits that come on people to leave. You have the power to tell cancer to go in the name of Jesus. Break that curse. Break that assignment. Break that greed. Break that anger spirit." You have the power over the demonic spirits.

When you have Jesus, you have all power and all authority and that is why Jesus said that it is important we get filled with the Baptism of the Holy Spirit. On the day of Pentecost, He gave them dynamite power. The demons are afraid of us. They tremble. They don't like us. We need to know who we are in Christ Jesus.

> **Little children, let no one deceive you. He who practices righteousness is righteous, just as He is righteous. He who sins is of the devil, for the devil has sinned from the beginning. For this purpose the Son of God was manifested, that He might destroy the works of the devil. Whoever has been born of God does not sin, for His seed remains in him; and he cannot sin, because he has been born of God. (1 John 3:7-9).**

When you are born of God, it doesn't mean you are never going to sin. But once you have asked Jesus Christ into your heart, you don't want to sin. The sin nature has been broken and you can overcome bad habits and sin where you could not before. Before Jesus, you did not have the strength to quit smoking or quit watching pornography, etc. Once Jesus is inside of you, He gives you the power and the strength to resist the devil and tell the devil where to go.

You can just roll over and let the devil beat you up but that is your choice. You don't have to because you have been given all power and authority over the devil. When Jesus comes into your heart, through faith in Jesus, He will break strongholds in your life.

How do you keep the devil away? By renewing your mind. If you don't read the Bible, pray, meditate on the Word and know the Word, the devil can deceive you. There are so many people being deceived in America. We need to watch out for false doctrines. We need to know that Jesus Christ was manifested to destroy the works of the devil.

> **I beseech you therefore, brethren, by the mercies of God, that you present your bodies a living sacrifice, holy, acceptable to God,**

which is your reasonable service. And do not be conformed to this world, but be transformed by the renewing of your mind, that you may prove what is that good and acceptable and perfect will of God. (Romans 12:1-2).

But now Christ is risen from the dead, and has become the firstfruits of those who have fallen asleep. For since by man came death, by Man also came the resurrection of the dead. For as in Adam all die, even so in Christ all shall be made alive. But each one in his own order: Christ the firstfruits, afterward those who are Christ's at His coming. Then comes the end, when He delivers the kingdom to God the Father, when He puts an end to all rule and all authority and power. For He must reign till He has put all enemies under His feet. The last enemy that will be destroyed is death. For "He has put all things under His feet." But when He says "all things are put under Him," it is evident that He who put all things under Him is excepted. Now when all things are made subject to Him, then the Son Himself will also be subject to Him

who put all things under Him, that God may be all in all. (1 Corinthians 15:20-28).

God has put Satan under His feet. He has destroyed all the works of the enemy, and we need to be wise.

How do demons get in people? How do you open doors for demons?

Nobody in their right mind is going to invite a demon in to torment them. But there are several ways that a demon can enter into somebody. I will talk about a few of those ways. Firstly, a demon can enter someone through distorted sex. Sex is not a sin, if we are having sex with our spouse. But the wrong kind of sex includes pornography, incest, rape, etc., and there is a spirit attached to each of these. There are pictures of our children on milk boxes and our missing children are in the newspapers and on the news because we have people possessed with demonic spirits who are not happy having normal sex. They want to have sex with a child. It never starts out with them having such a depraved desire. They may start out just doing a little thing wrong and then it doesn't satisfy. So they need to do more and it still doesn't satisfy. Pretty soon, they do a little more distorted sex and it still doesn't satisfy. So they start kidnapping children. There are those who kidnap children and sell to distorted men and women who are totally possessed by demons. There is a demonic force that is rampant around the world right now.

The devil worms his way in by maybe convincing someone to watch a little porn. It always starts out small because the devil is smart. He is not going to throw something big at you because he knows you will never do it. But if he starts out with something small and he keeps working at bringing something bigger, eventually you are doing what you thought you would never do.

Demon-Possessed Man

I was preaching in Montana and a lady came up to me after church and she said, "Would you go witness to my husband? He's not saved, and I really want him to get saved, and we're all going door-to-door Saturday anyway. So would you go to my husband and witness to him?"

I said, "Well, sure."

The pastor said to me as soon as she walked away, "Oh, you shouldn't have done that. Her husband is the worst man in town. He's terrible. He is so bad that he comes to my church service on Sunday."

I said, "Well, it can't be that bad if he comes to church."

Pastor said, "No. He doesn't come to church and come in church. He comes and parks as close to the front door as he can and blasts and honks his horn the whole time I'm in church. I have to go out there several times and tell him to stop blasting his horn. He said he has a right to do it. If that isn't enough, he put big billboards all across town saying that my church is a cult! And if that isn't enough, he made flyers and went all over different projects and housing places and put them out saying that my church is a cult because we speak in tongues. He's terrible."

I said, "But I promised her."

Pastor replied, "Well, I don't think you're going to get anybody to go with you."

Saturday came and I could not find anyone to go with me. We were supposed to go two by two. I said to the lady, his wife, "You stay at the church and pray. I'm going to go."

I went and I started five houses up from his house so I could tell him I was in the neighborhood. I finally got to his house. He had the door partly open so when I

knocked, it flew open and he says, "What do you want?"
He really scared me because he yelled at me.

I said, "Hi. I'm in the neighborhood. I've been going
from house to house and I want to talk with you."

"Are you a Christian?" He asked. "Are you from that
church up the street?"

I said, "No. I was at that church preaching."

He said, "Are you a member of that church?"

I said, "Nope. I go to Word of Faith Church." I was safe.
I was coming from that church but he didn't need to
know that.

He started talking loudly, "Would you look? Would you
just look? Come in."

I said, "What?"

He said, "Would you look at this pig sty? Look at it." He
had a shirt in his hands. "Do you see this shirt? I'm
trying to get ready to go to work. It isn't ironed. Do see
it? It's wrinkled. Where's my wife? Church. I can't get a
decent meal. When I do get a meal, she wants to pray
over it for fifteen minutes and preach a whole message

38

to me and I can't get her to shut up. She's driving me crazy."

I said, "Well, I'm really sorry to hear that." I was not doing a real good job of witnessing. "I'm really sorry. She should really treat you better. Did you say she was a Christian?"

He said, "Yes."

I said, "Well, then, she should be loving you and treating you better."

"Well, she's not. I've about had it with her," he said. "So I don't want to go to heaven because she's going to be there nagging at me forever. So I told Satan he could have my soul."

I have no idea what happened to me at that point. The next thing I did was grab him by the bathrobe he was wearing and I was shaking him and saying, "You don't know what you just did! Hell is terrible. You don't want to make a deal with Satan."

When I finally came to my senses, I was like, "Oh, my God." I was looking at him embarrassed. So I straightened his collar and kind of patted his little collar down.

He looked at me and said, "Get out! Just get out of my house."

I started to leave and all of a sudden he just turned into a monster and started growling. I should have had somebody with me.

He said, "I said get out of my house."

I was walking backwards, and I said, "You really should not have done that."

He said, "I don't want to hear what you have to say." He folded his fist, and swung his hand back and he punched me in the jaw with every bit of strength he had. He did it three times and I remember thinking, "Why am I not knocked out? Why am I not on the floor?"

He kept saying, "Now, I said get out!"

He hit me three times and I never felt it. He was getting ready to hit me again and I said, "You touch me one more time and my angels are going to pick you up and throw you into that wall. You got it?"

He said, "I got it."

I left. I went back to the church and talked to his wife. I told her that he had demons inside of him.

The pastor of the church, who was about 5' 5" tall, called me later that week. He said, "What in the world did you do to that man?"

I said, "Why, Pastor?"

He said, "Well, he came over to the church, and this is awesome. He was so furious at me and he said, 'You sent that lady to my house!'"

The man's wife went home with one of my books ("Let's Go Fishing") and there was a picture of me on the back. When the man asked his wife where she had been, she showed him my picture and said, "I've been at this "Let's Go Fishing" seminar with this lady here." He recognized my face and went to the pastor and said, "How dare you?"

A few weeks later, the man called the pastor and said, "Pastor, you have to come over to my house." Pastor told him, "Okay."

Pastor called me to tell me what happened. He said, "I went over to his house and started sharing Jesus with him and he started to swing at me, like he did you."

41

I said, "Well, Pastor, what did you do?"

He said, "Well, I figured if I was going to get knocked out, I might as well go in glory. So I started dancing around his living room and speaking in tongues. The guy just looked at me and said, 'You're nuts! Just like that lady that was here. Get out of here! Just get out of here. You Christians are nuts.'" So pastor left.

A few weeks later, the man called pastor again. The devil will keep working on you little by little to get you to do things you thought you would never do. The husband called the pastor again and he said, "I need to come over. I won't hurt you. Please let me come. I don't know what's happening to me. But ever since I told Satan he could have my soul, I've become a man that I do not respect. I hate men who hit their wives. I've been beating my wife pretty regular lately and I have always hated men who touch women. I tried to beat up your evangelist and now I'm hitting my wife all the time. I'm not the same person since I gave my soul to Satan. Something's not right with me."

The pastor said to me on the phone, "He humbled himself and I got three or four guys from the church and we cast devils out of him and he accepted Jesus Christ and was filled with the Baptism of the Holy Spirit. He's a regular member of the church and he put a big ad in the paper saying, 'Please, everybody all the flyers I'd put out are wrong. It's a good church.' He changed his billboard to say, "Go to this church" instead of, "It's a Cult.'"

When you are possessed by demons, you will do things: kill people, bomb up buildings, shoot up people, kill babies, etc. You will do things you thought you would never do because it is not you doing it. You have allowed an evil spirit to influence you and take you over. We have to be careful and guard ourselves even as Christians because Jesus paid the price for us.

Giving thanks to the Father who has qualified us to be partakers of the inheritance of the saints in the light. He has delivered us from the power of darkness and conveyed us into the kingdom of the Son of His love, in whom we have redemption through His blood, the forgiveness of sins. (Colossians 1:12-14).

And you, being dead in your trespasses and the uncircumcision of your flesh, He has made alive together with Him, having forgiven you all trespasses, having wiped out the handwriting of requirements that was

**against us, which was contrary to us. And He
has taken it out of the way, having nailed it to
the cross. Having disarmed principalities and
powers, He made a public spectacle of them,
triumphing over them in it. (Colossians 2:13-
15).**

When Jesus died on the cross, He triumphed over all
sins. He nailed them to the cross.

They Didn't Know What They Were Doing

When I was born, I was a nice person for a long time.
But then, my stepdad started sexually abusing me at the
age of seven. I was traumatized. Because of that trauma,
my personality was altered. So I no longer had the
personality that God had ordained for me. I became this
bitter, hateful little girl that was defiant. I hated my
stepdad and wanted to kill him. I opened the door to a
demon of murder. I was so full of rage from being
sexually abused that when I was mad, I would break
everything in the house. I would drive a car and jump
out of the car. I did some bad things.

Just before I was saved, I started doing drugs. Before I
was saved, they had to cast devils out of me. I was set
free from demons, but evidently, some demons were

trying to get back into me. We have to watch because another way that demons come in is from bad teaching from the pulpit or letting people pray for you when they don't know what they are doing. There are doctrines of demons.

There was a seminar they were doing on inner healing. I was a fairly new Christian at that time. I was delivered but I was only saved for five or six years. I already asked my stepdad to forgive me for the hatred I had towards him. But they still wanted to do inner healing on me so I went.

I started to think about when I was seven. I had blanked my mind out so much that I wasn't in control of my mind anymore. I was opening the door for demons. It is amazing how this happened. I saw when I was sexually abused the first time while out in the woods. All of a sudden, my stepdad was coming down on top of me. But instead of it being my stepdad, it turned into a demon that came inside me. I started screaming and shaking.

I said, "You guys don't know what you're doing with this crazy stuff." I made them stop. We don't need to dig up our past to be healed. We have the Holy Spirit who will bring up what we need to deal with when He thinks we are ready. We don't have to go digging up old memories because we are stirring up old demons.

So I had to do deliverance on myself because that demon was tormenting my brain. I told them all to get out and I spent time praising God and getting in the Word of God because I realized that I was stupid to let people mess around with me. I don't let everybody pray for me. Don't let everybody lay hands on you. You don't know what kind of spirits they have. You don't know what they do. You don't know their lifestyle. Be careful.

Demonic Doorways

Demons can enter through fortune telling. I was scheduled to preach in Reno, Nevada. I never go shopping just before I preach on a Sunday. That is ridiculous. I am a minister of the gospel of Jesus Christ. My job is to pray, work on my message and then go to the church and be ready to preach and pray for the people. So I was praying and getting ready to go to the church. It was a night service. I had already done Sunday morning service. While getting ready, the Holy Spirit said, "Go to Mervyns." It was a women's clothing store.

I said, "No, no, no. I don't do that. I'm going to go straight to the church and keep praying."

It kept getting stronger, "Go to Mervyns."

I said, "Lord, it's Sunday. I don't ever shop on Sundays."

But I kept hearing this small still voice saying, "Go to Mervyns." I know His voice. It was the Holy Spirit and I thought it was really strange that I had to go to a clothing store on my way to the Sunday night service. I was already dressed for church so I went. It was enroute to the church where I was going anyway.

I went to Mervyns' clothing store. I heard the Holy Spirit say, "Get something and go in the dressing room."

I said, "I don't want to buy anything."

I heard the Holy Spirit again say, "Get some clothes and go in the dressing room." So I just grabbed a few things off the rack and went to the dressing room. They had a little booth at the back of the dressing room area and a lady giving out tickets. I was directed to an available room. I was not planning to try on anything. They probably didn't fit anyway. I had just grabbed something.

I sat quietly for a moment. I heard this conversation in the next room between two ladies who were trying on clothes. One lady said, "I don't know what's wrong with me."

The other lady asked, "What do you mean?"

"Well, yesterday, I went to a fortune teller. I saw there was a sign for discounted fortune telling, so I went to the fortune teller, and this lady shared my fortune, but ever since then I've been petrified. I noticed something's bothering me. I feel like something terrible is going to happen to me. I don't know. I think I'm going to die or something." She sounded really panicked.

When I heard the door open, I came out and said, "Excuse me" to the lady who had been to the fortune teller. There were about five or six other ladies around. I said to her, "Let me talk to you. It's very important that I talk to you. You opened the door to demonic forces." I shared with them that demons come in because we opened the door and she said, "Oh, please tell me how to shut the door?"

All of a sudden there were 10 or 15 people gathered around and listening to me share. I said, "You could all get hurt. The enemy is always trying to get in, but the only way you're going to get saved and be okay is to accept Jesus."

One of the ladies asked, "How do we do it?"

I shared with them how to accept Jesus and they all prayed and asked Jesus into their hearts. That is why I was there. When I was through, I took off to go to church. I had written down their names and numbers and I gave them to the pastor. That was the only time ever in my life that I went shopping just before church. But I wasn't really shopping, I was on an assignment.

Another way demons can come in is by us taking home an item from a foreign country that has a curse on it. One thing we should do is go through our houses and get the things out that should not be there. I used to have fancy Indian jewelry and the Lord told me to get rid of it. The Holy Spirit will direct you on what to get rid of.

I went to Alaska one time and they had totem poles. They were pretty with some fancy artwork. The Lord told me to get rid of it. Those represent other gods.

Drugs is another way demons come in. Drugs open you up to demons. Not just people being drug addicts, but prescription drugs. Prescription drugs are really an epidemic state in our country. They will cause you to think demonic thoughts. Anti-depressants are an open doorway for Satan.

There are different ways that demons come in. They come in through curses, unforgiveness, abuse, sexual abuse, bad teaching, occults and cursed objects.

We need to enforce the kingdom of our Lord and Savior, Jesus Christ, and take authority over demonic spirits that are hindering people. We need to recognize where demons come from, and not be ignorant of their methods. If you are having trouble sleeping, anger issues that show up randomly, unforgiveness, etc., it doesn't mean you are possessed, but you are tormented by demons. All sickness came from the fall. There was no sickness or disease until after the fall. Once we are able to identify the presence of demons, we need to know what to do next.

We have the power to set people free in the name of Jesus.

Chapter 3
Preparing For Battle

Have you ever tried witnessing to a loved one who has not accepted the Lord Jesus as Savior? Do you have friends, relatives, neighbors or aquantances who you have tried to share Jesus with, and they won't come to Jesus? These cases may require more than just being a witness. We need to learn how to set the captives free. Unless they are free, it will be hard for them to make the decision to serve Jesus.

We want to learn how to share the gospel, how to pray and how to go forth so we can see people come into the kingdom of God because we are running out of time. We need to see people come to Jesus Christ because hell and heaven are real places and we want our loved ones, family, relatives and neighbors in heaven.

God wants us to be wise in what we do. Let's read what the Scriptures say about our mandate as a church:

And as you go, preach, saying, 'The kingdom of heaven is at hand.' Heal the sick, cleanse the lepers, raise the dead, cast out demons. Freely you have received, freely give." (Matthew 10:7-8).

The word which God sent to the children of Israel, preaching peace through Jesus Christ—He is Lord of all— that word you know, which was proclaimed throughout all Judea, and began from Galilee after the baptism which John preached: how God anointed Jesus of Nazareth with the Holy Spirit and with power, who went about doing good and healing all who were oppressed by the devil, for God was with Him. (Acts 10:36-38).

When Jesus was walking the earth, He knew He had the power to tell devils where to go. He knew He had the power to tell epileptics to be set free from demonic forces. He knew He could say to the spirit of deafness, "You spirit of deafness, go" and the deaf would be healed. He knew how to pray for the blind and see the lame walk. God is saying we need to recognize that there are demonic forces holding our loved ones back from coming to Jesus.

The Spirit Of Discernment

Marty and I were scheduled to preach at a church up in the mountains in Idaho. After the meeting, we went into a little convenience store. I shared Jesus with a few people and I was handing out tracts to everybody in the convenience store. The tract had a simple message that Jesus loves us and we were running out of time so they needed to accept Jesus as Lord.

When we were finished, and got back in our car, a man was following us. He was on my side of the car and Marty was sitting in the driver's seat. The man started pounding on the window, so I rolled the window down and said, "What can I do for you?"

The man said, "No, you're not going to get away with what you're doing."

I said, "What did I do wrong?"

He said, "You handed me this little piece of paper that tells me that Jesus loves me and Jesus wants me in heaven. So you're not going to get away with just handing me a piece of paper. I want to know how do I get to heaven."

We shared the plan of salvation with him and then I said, "Hold my hand and I'll lead you in a prayer to receive Jesus."

The man could not pray the prayer. Each time I said, "Say Jesus," he could not. Whenever I said, "Repeat after me. Pray and ask Jesus...", the man just groaned. There are deaf and dumb spirits that block people from hearing the gospel. When people are hurt, wounded and scared, the demons come in no matter what you say to them. Instead of them hearing it, they reject it and come against you. But it is not them opposing you but the spirit in them that is blocking them from hearing the truth. The demons know that the truth will set captives free.

Marty, who has a spirit of discernment, got out of the car and walked around to my side. He stood beside the man and started praying for him. Then he placed his hand on the man, who was a Native American. Marty said, "Satan, you deaf and dumb spirit that is trying to control his mouth so he cannot say Jesus and he cannot hear the truth, I take authority over you in the name of Jesus Christ of Nazareth. You go from this man now in the name of Jesus."

The man started crying. We asked him if he was ready to pray the prayer and he said yes and the man accepted Jesus into his heart. We have the authority over the demons that are over our loved ones, children, etc. We must pray and ask the Holy Spirit, "What is the spirit that's holding them?" The Lord will reveal the demons to you, whether it is an antichrist spirit or a hurt spirit or a wounded spirit. God will show you because He has given you power just like Jesus has power.

Jesus had power and He went about doing good and healing all who were oppressed of the devil. He knows that the demons don't rest. Satan comes to steal, kill, and destroy. He wants to kill, steal, and destroy your family. He wants to steal your joy. You will not have joy if your grandson is out there doing drugs and not sitting beside you in church on a Sunday. It is an awesome feeling to have your family members on fire for the Lord. That is what we desire, but we must fight against the forces that come against us. God gave us the gifts of the Holy Spirit which is spoken of in 1 Corinthians chapter 12. One of those gifts is discerning of spirits.

Marty Has The Gift Of Discernment

Marty operates very strongly in the gift of discerning of spirits. I found this out just a few months after being married to him. What happened was, I had to get a new accountant to run the ministry, so I asked a pastor friend of mine and he said, "Well, my sister's an accountant and she does accounting. She is really good and she just got filled with the Holy Spirit and she is a member of our church."

I trusted the pastor's recommendation so I hired her and she started working for us at the Channel of Love Ministries. She was responsible for taking care of all the money coming in and she was also going to handle our newsletters and just about everything.

We were living in Washington and we would fly to Florida for six months at a time until we actually moved to Florida as newlyweds. I remember Marty saying to me one day, "You need to check on that accountant that you have. Something's not right."

I was in ministry long before I was married. So in my mind, I was thinking, "Who are you? You just got married to me and I've been in ministry 15 years and now you're going to tell me?"

Sometimes we need to listen to our spouses. Marty said, "I'm telling you something's wrong."

So I said, "You know what, Honey, I didn't know you had a critical spirit. You just don't like her."

He said, "Why would I not like her? I only met her once."

I said, "I don't know, but you have a critical spirit. You just don't like her."

A few months passed, and he said it again, "Honey, I'm telling you, something's really wrong with your accountant."

I kept ignoring him until six months later when we went home and we found out that she embezzled all the money that came into the ministry. She lost our entire list with names and addresses of people we send newsletters to. We had built relationships with many of our supporters for fifteen years. She said the lists just disappeared. She also did not fill out our corporation forms. As a result, we almost lost our whole corporation. My husband was nice and he did not say, "I told you so." He had discerned what was going on in Washington State (3,000 miles away). We need that gift that my husband has. He just needs to be around somebody for a little while and he can discern when there is a bad spirit there.

Demonic spirits are real and they are out there. That accountant was trying to destroy the ministry. I was asked to press charges, but I didn't. There were already nine other people who hired her as their accountant and they were all pressing charges. She was charged and sentenced to twenty years in prison for embezzling all those different businesses. I was the only ministry who let it go because the Bible says we should not sue a brother or sister in the Lord. But I learned a lesson, so when my husband says something now, I listen better. My husband was so persistent in trying to warn me and I wasn't very nice to him. I had to ask my husband to forgive me for not trusting him when he tried to warn me. Now I trust the Holy Spirit in him.

We need to be more aware of the demonic spirits that are around us, not just to hinder our families, but also be mindful that there are spirits out to destroy our marriages.

Learn To Forgive

Marty and I were traveling across the Bay Bridge that goes into San Francisco because we were scheduled to minister at a church. We were getting along fine, listening to praise tapes and worshiping on our way to the church service, when suddenly all hell broke loose.

Marty was mad at me, and I was mad at him. He was raising his voice and I was raising my voice. By the time we arrived at the church service, we were both mad at each other.

I was the preacher for that Sunday morning and I was really upset. The pastor welcomed us and took us to a back room. Instead of praying, the pastor and others from the church were in the prayer room talking about a football game. They wanted to know what the scores were. I thought to myself, "Right now we could use some prayer." We proceeded to go into the sanctuary. We still did not pray.

It was a large church of about 500 or 600 people. We walked out into the auditorium and were led to the stage. Everybody was staring at us. Marty was sitting beside me. He was always the first to bring peace, not me. For years, he was always the one to say, "I am sorry" first. So, we were on the platform, and I was thinking, "Lord, I'm very upset. How am I going to flow in the gifts? How am I going to preach? You said, 'Don't let the sun go down on your wrath and don't have anger in you' and I will have to get up in that pulpit and be anointed!"

I looked over at Marty and he looked back at me and winked. I reached out my hand to him and he reached for my hand. He squeezed my hand and I knew he had forgiven me. So I said, "I'm sorry." I melted.

He said, "I'm sorry too."

No one was looking at us because they were all worshiping.

We had a visitation that morning. People were falling out under the power of the Holy Spirit all over the place. Even the guy on the piano fell off his seat. People were healed and delivered. Wonderful things were happening and a little boy came up. He was about five years old and he said, "I saw a great, big angel over the piano." That was where the guy fell off the piano bench.

If we did not take authority and ask God to forgive us, we would have hindered what God wanted to do. The demons will always try to cause friction in a marriage. The demons want to destroy all marriages. They want to take your money, your house, etc. They want to steal everything you have and put sickness on you because they came to destroy.

After the service was over, we went to lunch with the pastor and had a long talk with him. He said he had pastored several churches in different cities and San Francisco was the hardest city he had ever preached in.

He said there were principalities and strong demon forces over the city of San Francisco. When Marty and I got back to our hotel room after lunch, we talked together and realized that it was right when we reached the bridge to come into San Francisco that we started arguing and fighting. We realized it wasn't us but a demon force causing friction between us. So we learned this lesson from that event that it is very important for you to also know that there are powers of darkness and principalities over areas where we go, and we have the power to pull down strongholds and principalities and be aware of the devices of the enemy.

Satan is mad because he used to be in heaven. He was close to God, but he was lifted up in pride. He was so lifted up in pride that he caused a church split in heaven and a third of the angels were cast out of heaven to earth. They are here and they are trying to take as many people to hell as they can.

Know your authority in Christ Jesus.

Chapter 4
Demons Recognize Authority

Then they went into Capernaum, and immediately on the Sabbath He entered the synagogue and taught. And they were astonished at His teaching, for He taught them as one having authority, and not as the scribes. Now there was a man in their synagogue with an unclean spirit. And he cried out, saying, "Let us alone! What have we to do with You, Jesus of Nazareth? Did You come to destroy us? I know who You are—the Holy One of God!" But Jesus rebuked him, saying, "Be quiet, and come out of him!" And when the unclean spirit had convulsed him and cried out with a loud voice, he came out of him. Then they were all amazed, so that they questioned among themselves, saying, "What is this? What new doctrine is this?

For with authority He commands even the unclean spirits, and they obey Him." And immediately His fame spread throughout all the region around Galilee. (Mark 1:21-28).

When we cast demonic spirits out of people, they are free. When they are free, then we can share the love of Jesus with them. They need to be set free from demonic forces before they can call on the name of Jesus. So we need to take authority over whatever is binding them.

In the Scripture in Mark 1:21-28, we see the demon talking to Jesus. The demon said, "We know who you are. You are the Holy One. You are Jesus." The devils know Jesus. When people tell me that they know Jesus, it is not an indication that they are saved. Even the devils know who Jesus is and they are definitely not saved.

Everyone must have a personal relationship with Jesus. We can't just know about Jesus. We must have a personal relationship with Christ.

Now as soon as they had come out of the synagogue, they entered the house of Simon and Andrew, with James and John. But

Simon's wife's mother lay sick with a fever, and they told Him about her at once. So He came and took her by the hand and lifted her up, and immediately the fever left her. And she served them. At evening, when the sun had set, they brought to Him all who were sick and those who were demon-possessed. (Mark 1:29-32).

There are different kinds of miracles. The whole city was gathered together at the door and Jesus healed many who were sick of various diseases, and cast out many demons. He did not allow the demons to speak because they knew Him. We don't need to wrestle with demons all the time.

Freedom From A Whisper

We do evangelism schools across the country and we were in one of those schools doing ministry. While praying for people one night, there was a man who had a demon in him and the demon was manifesting. I started yelling at the demon. I was yelling at the devil, "Come out in the name of Jesus." Marty was on the sound board. He came down from the sound board, walked over to where I was, and he said, "Excuse me, Honey." He went over to the guy I was yelling at and whispered in his ear. The guy falls on the ground, foaming at the mouth and flip-flopping on the ground as the demons came out of him. I was amazed because I was yelling at this guy for over ten minutes and the demons would not leave. Marty whispered in the man's ear, and the demons came out.

After the meeting, Marty said to me, "Honey, you don't have to yell at demons. They know if you have authority."

Jesus told demons to be quiet. We don't have to yell at demons. They know if we have authority. I said to Marty, "I like yelling at them."

He asked, "Why do you like to yell at them? All you're doing is hurting your throat and vocal cords."

I said, "Because the devils had me bound for years. The devil took over my body. I was demon-possessed and the Lord set me free. The devil tried to kill me, and the Lord set me free. Therefore, I am really mad at the demons and I like screaming at them."

He said, "But you don't have to. I just whispered in his ear and said, 'Come out in the name of Jesus.'" The devil knows your authority in Christ.

Joan's Deliverance

Before I was saved, I had a neighbor who witnessed to me. Other people had been witnessing to me for years, but I would not listen to them. The reason I did not listen to them was because I had a deaf and dumb spirit. I did not know I had a deaf and dumb spirit. I had a demon in me and no matter who told me about Jesus, it was blocked. I didn't know I had a demon in me.

Most people who are possessed by demons don't know that they are possessed. They do certain things, for example, have a violent temper or lie or cheat and that is really not their personality. The devil takes over and makes you not be who God really meant for you to be.

Anyway, my neighbor started witnessing to me and telling me about Jesus but I could never hear her. I was studying to be a Mormon and Jehovah's Witness and all these different movements, and this neighbor started telling me about Jesus. She shared the gospel with me for nine months. One day she asked me if I would go with her to a meeting. I told her okay. I decided to go with the hope that she would leave me alone afterwards.

We went to the meeting. When the meeting was closing out, she said to me, "Would you go up and let the evangelist pray for you?"

I said, "No way. I don't want that man touching me." I did not know that was the devil stopping me from going. The devil did not want me going near that evangelist because he would see and know what was going on and make that demon come out. I didn't know that. So, I left the meeting. If you are at a meeting and notice a non-Christian always leaving before the altar call, it is usually a spirit in them.

I left the meeting and went to the car because I wanted to get out of there. The anointing was so strong. My neighbor came out to the car and she deceived me. She said, "Come back into the meeting."

I said, "No, I don't want to be around that evangelist."

God tells us to be wise in how we do things. So she was being wise and a little deceptive. All of a sudden, she said she felt like she was about to faint.

I said, "What's wrong?" I was sitting in my car with the car engine on because I was going to leave.

She said, "I feel kind of sick. Would you walk me back in so I can get back okay?"

So, I said, "Oh, sure."

I turned the car off, locked the doors and walked with her back inside.

She said, "Can you take me up there to the evangelist so he can pray for me?"

I said, "Yeah, sure." I was not thinking about me anymore. I was thinking about her. So I walked with her to where the evangelist was, and said to him, "She's not feeling good and I have no idea what happened."

The evangelist suddenly turned to me and said, "What are you into?"

I said, "What?"

He was yelling at me, "You're in a cult." He was screaming at me and I was thinking, "What did I do?"

He started praying for me and I suddenly felt sick. So I said to him, "You need to stop praying for me because I feel sick. I'm going to throw up on you."

He asked, "You feel like throwing up?"

69

I answered, "Yes."

He said, "Good." He grabbed me and dragged me down the hall, out into the lobby and into the women's bathroom. The women who were in the bathroom got up and ran out because a man was now in the bathroom. He said to me, "There's the toilet."

He put me over the toilet and said, "You want to get sick now? I'm going to keep praying for you. Go ahead, there's the toilet. Throw up." My neighbor and another lady was also there standing behind me.

The evangelist said, "I said come out."

I was thinking, "What's he trying to get out? I don't know." I was just a Catholic girl.

He kept saying, "I said come out." Then he said, "Satan, I command you in the name of Jesus to come out."

I knew nothing about devils and I did not know about Jesus. Suddenly, I felt something clawing inside of me. It felt like something was in me and did not want to come out, so it was digging inside of me, not wanting to come out. The evangelist said, "I said in Jesus' name come out."

I don't know what happened to me. All I remember was that I changed. I remember thinking, "If he says that name Jesus one more time, I am going to kill him." I was not a murderer so how could I be having that thought?

He said, "In Jesus' name..." I turned and looked at him. I don't know what I looked like but I bet it was pretty bad.

The two women were looking at me strangely. I heard when one of them said, "Oh, my God. What's gotten into her?" The two women tried to hold me. I was a size ten then, and I grabbed one of the women and had her pinned to the toilet wall. I pushed the other woman aside and I went after the evangelist to kill him. It was not me, but the demon in me. I had demons in me because I was doing drugs. I was sexually abused so a demon came inside of me. The Lord showed me that a demon came in when I was seven because of being sexually abused by my stepdad. I was full of hate. So when the devil knew I was full of hate, a demon came in and more demons kept coming until there were probably seven to ten demons. I don't know how many demons I had.

The evangelist never gave up. He said, "I said come out." I felt something ripping inside me as if it was clawing to

71

try to hold on while it was coming out. When the demons came out, I felt limp. There was no strength left in my body. The evangelist held me there in that bathroom and I was crying because I did not know what was going on. I know I tried to kill the evangelist. I was crying and the evangelist held me and said, "It's okay. You're all right."

I have no idea exactly what that evangelist did, but he made a mistake. We cannot cast the devil out of someone and not fill that space with Jesus.

> **When an unclean spirit goes out of a man, he goes through dry places, seeking rest; and finding none, he says, 'I will return to my house from which I came.' And when he comes, he finds it swept and put in order. Then he goes and takes with him seven other spirits more wicked than himself, and they enter and dwell there; and the last state of that man is worse than the first. (Luke 11:24-26).**

The evangelist did not ask me if I knew Jesus Christ as my Lord and Savior. I was not saved. So he said, "You're okay" and he held me for a while. He prayed a little prayer but he did not get me saved.

I got in my car and drove off. Now, let me share what demons do. Satan comes to steal, kill, and destroy. It felt like someone else was driving my car. I had a few miles to go before I was home, and the car was swerving and trying to go into the sides of the freeway to kill me. Satan was trying to kill me and the demons were trying to get back in me. I looked in my mirror and I saw a demon. He had a black shape and beady red eyes.

I had told my neighbor that I could not read so she had bought me the New Testament Bible on cassettes. I had them on the front seat of the car and there was one already in the player so I pressed the play button. Satan cannot stand the Word of God. Once the tape started to play, the demon left. Whenever you feel like you are being tormented, play an audio version of the Word of God. Play it low, and leave it on all night. You can also use praise tapes. If you think there is a demon in your house, walk through your house and command every spirit not of God out. Do not go to foreign countries and bring strange items home. We need to be careful what we do so as not to draw demonic spirits to ourselves.

When I got home, I went to bed. The demon showed up again because the Word of God was not on. It stood over my bed looking at me. It said, "You're going to die." I did not know better, so I thought that I could outthink that demonic spirit. So I said, "No, no, no."

The demonic spirit kept saying, "You're going to die."

Soon, my lips started to say, "I am going to die."

The devil can work on your mind and start putting thoughts in your mind, for example, "I'm no good. I'll never make it. I will be sick. I think I have cancer." If he can get you to agree with what he is saying, he will have you where he wants you. Never agree with the devil. He is the father of lies.

> **You are of your father the devil, and the desires of your father you want to do. He was a murderer from the beginning, and does not stand in the truth, because there is no truth in him. When he speaks a lie, he speaks from his own resources, for he is a liar and the father of it. (John 8:44).**

Why would we listen to a liar?

The devil was lying to me and saying, "You're going to die." I was whispering, "I'm going to die."

Then the demon started to say, "You're dying." He was trying to pull me deeper into his deceptive web. Soon, my lips were saying, "I'm dying."

After a few moments of trying to fight this as a non-Christian, the demon started to say, "You're dead." Satan's playground is in our minds.

I crossed my hands across my chest and the demon said, "You're dead." I saw all three of my children coming in the morning before they went to school and screaming after seeing their mother in bed dead. I saw myself dead. I was visualizing my death. I really believed that I was going to be dead in two seconds.

Suddenly, the demon jumped on top of me and started choking me. I knew I was going to be dead. I didn't know how to fight the devil.

Christians should know how to fight the devil. The devil is trying to steal our country, our peace, our children and trying to bring in gay marriages and abortions. Satan is behind it all. He is trying to bring us down. There is a plot for a one world order so Satan can be inside the Antichrist. We need to be aware of the devices of the enemy. We can't just go through life and not know what is going on.

The demon was choking me. I didn't know how to fight the devil. I didn't know the Bible. I was illiterate. I didn't go to a church that told me about demons. I knew nothing. But God is faithful, especially when we are a baby. I don't know how else to explain it. I was gasping for air. I couldn't talk. I was weak, but then a word came out of my mouth, "Jesus." I could not say His name out loud. It was just a whisper, "Jesus." Just a faint sound, "Jesus." When I said that name, the thing loosened it's grip on me so I could speak a little louder. I said, "Jesus" again and he let go. Then I yelled, "Jesus" and my room became brighter than the sun. I passed out under the presence of God.

When I woke up the next morning, my children had already gone off to school. I got up and drank some coffee and the Lord showed me a vision of my whole life. I was now communicating clearly with God which confirmed that I really had a demonic spirit that was blocking me from hearing anything about Jesus. In the vision, I saw someone talking to me when I was five years old. I then saw someone witnessing to me when I was a teenager, and when I was in my twenties. I also saw my neighbor who had been witnessing to me for months. Everything that was blocked up was coming up to the surface. I jumped up, ran to my bedroom and dropped to my knees in prayer, "Lord, You were there all the time. Oh, God, You were there all the time. Lord Jesus, come into my heart." I was changed.

We need to be aware of the spirits that are blocking our loved ones from coming to Jesus, messing up marriages and finances. Jesus gave us a mandate to, "Go set the captives free."

> **Later He appeared to the eleven as they sat at the table; and He rebuked their unbelief and hardness of heart, because they did not believe those who had seen Him after He had risen. And He said to them, "Go into all the world and preach the gospel to every creature." (Mark 16:14-15).**

If we are going to preach the gospel, we need to preach the whole gospel. The whole gospel is that Jesus saves and He gives us life abundantly. Jesus heals all sicknesses and diseases and we have power over demons. Jesus doesn't want us to be poor. He broke every curse. He became a curse so we don't have to be under any curses. Jesus came to set us free.

We need to go out into the world, pray and see the gift of discerning of spirits in operation and take authority over demonic spirits so we can see people who are bound come to know Jesus. We have the power to take authority over cancer and tumors and epilepsy and command those spirits to come out. We have that power because Jesus gave us that power.

> He who believes and is baptized will be saved; but he who does not believe will be condemned. And these signs will follow those who believe: In My name they will cast out demons; they will speak with new tongues; they will take up serpents; and if they drink anything deadly, it will by no means hurt them; they will lay hands on the sick, and they will recover. (Mark 16:16-18).

God wants us to know that we have power. He has shared that fact so many times in Scripture.

> For though we walk in the flesh, we do not war according to the flesh. For the weapons of our warfare are not carnal but mighty in God for pulling down strongholds, casting down arguments and every high thing that exalts itself against the knowledge of God, bringing every thought into captivity to the obedience of Christ, and being ready to punish all

disobedience when your obedience is fulfilled. (2 Corinthians 10:3-6).

We have the power to cast down bad thoughts: lustful thoughts, cheating thoughts, cheating on our taxes thoughts, etc. Those thoughts are not your thoughts. The devil is putting them in your mind so you need to know how to take authority over those thoughts. The devil is always shooting arrows at you to try and bring you down. A very simple thought like, "You don't need to go to church today" can have devastating effects on your Christian growth. You need to tell Satan that he is a liar. You must be in the house of God. You must be busy building His kingdom. Paul tells us how we can stay strong.

I beseech you therefore, brethren, by the mercies of God, that you present your bodies a living sacrifice, holy, acceptable to God, which is your reasonable service. And do not be conformed to this world, but be transformed by the renewing of your mind, that you may prove what is that good and acceptable and perfect will of God. (Romans 12:1-2).

We have talked about how we can open doors to demonic spirits. We need to learn how to shut those doors.

The Past Can Come Back To Haunt Us

I was preaching in Texas and a pastor friend of mine had a twin brother who was tormented by nightmares. The demons would come and try to choke him. He was a Spirit-filled Christian so the demons were not in him, but they still tormented him to the point that he couldn't sleep. He would be up all night because of the tormenting dreams. Satan was stealing his rest. He went to work tired and he was always too tired to read the Bible.

My pastor friend said, "Let's get him on the phone." So we called him and had him on speakerphone. He was in California and I was in Texas with his brother. He wanted to be free so he could get a good night's sleep. We started praying. We started to operate in the spirit of discernment. I asked him, "Did you ever use an Ouija board?"

He said, "I don't think so."

I said, "Holy Spirit, bring to remembrance."

Suddenly, he said, "Oh, yes. I did a Ouija board when I was in my twenties and then I also did witchcraft. Oh, yes. I did that when I was young, a teenager." He was now a grown man.

Any sin can be an open door for demons, and we need to close those doors in order to be free. So, we took authority. I said, "You ask God to forgive you for doing the Ouija board. You ask God to forgive you for the witchcraft." He asked God's forgiveness and then we prayed for him until those demon spirits left. He was totally set free. He called us the next day and told us he had a wonderful night's sleep.

One month later, he was still sleeping soundly. He told us from the very next day that the demons were gone. He had put up with the torment for so many years, and now he is free. We have a tendency to put up with a lot of demonic oppression, but there comes a time when we must say, "Enough is enough" and deal with that demon force.

The devil has no right to torment you. He has no right to torment your children. You need to start asking the Holy Spirit to show you what is keeping your children, grandchildren, neighbors and loved ones from coming to the Lord. It is time for you and those you are sharing the gospel with to be free. If you have accepted Jesus and are filled with the Holy Spirit, you have the power.

So pray for the Lord to use you. Go in God's power and set the captives free.

Chapter 5
Principles For Setting The
Captives Free

When we learn to get ourselves out of the way and let the Holy Ghost take over, we will see amazing miracles. We need to know the principles that will lead to freedom. These are principles that we should also be teaching to our children so they know how to overcome the devil and move forward with the work that God has ordained for all of us to do.

On the same day, when evening had come, He said to them, "Let us cross over to the other side." Now when they had left the multitude, they took Him along in the boat as He was. And other little boats were also with Him. And a great windstorm arose, and the waves beat into the boat, so that it was already filling. But He was in the stern, asleep on a pillow. And they awoke Him and said to Him, "Teacher, do You not care that we are

perishing?" Then He arose and rebuked the wind, and said to the sea, "Peace, be still!" And the wind ceased and there was a great calm. But He said to them, "Why are you so fearful? How is it that you have no faith?" And they feared exceedingly, and said to one another, "Who can this be, that even the wind and the sea obey Him!" (Mark 4:35-41).

Jesus was in no way bothered by the storm. Jesus was the one who told the disciples to go to the other side. He must have known that a storm was waiting. God will sometimes allow us to go through some storms in life. We have all been there, but you need to know that Jesus will never leave nor forsake you. When you are in the midst of a storm, you can cry out to God and God will always get you to the other side. He will get you through the storm, through the situation. God will always take you from point A to point B to point C because when you are in the perfect will of God, He orders your footsteps according to His Word. He will make sure that you get where you are supposed to go. He knows there is a miracle waiting on the other side. We may not know who the miracle is for. Sometimes, the miracle is for us, but there are times God will order your steps and take you to a particular place at the right time for someone else's miracle.

God wants to use us to cast out devils, take care of people, pray for the sick, see people saved and delivered. Whatever God's perfect plan for your life is, you must be ready to go but the devil will try to stop you from getting to your divine appointment.

So, Jesus and His disciples were on a boat and the devil stirred up a storm to see if he could sink the boat before Jesus and the apostles got across. There was a miracle waiting on the other side.

> **Then they came to the other side of the sea, to the country of the Gadarenes. And when He had come out of the boat, immediately there met Him out of the tombs a man with an unclean spirit, who had his dwelling among the tombs; and no one could bind him, not even with chains, because he had often been bound with shackles and chains. And the chains had been pulled apart by him, and the shackles broken in pieces; neither could anyone tame him. (Mark 5:1-4).**

This man had super human strength because of the demons inside him. He broke chains and he even cut himself.

There was a time when Marty worked as a roofer. One day he met the daughter of the homeowner whose roof he was repairing. She was a teenage girl who took razor blades and was always cutting her arms and nobody could stop her. There are demonic spirits that cause people to cut themselves.

Some Christians believe in body-piercings and tattoos, but I believe it is demonic. Some people go to the extreme with piercings that they have some great big hooks protruding from different parts of their bodies. That is demonic.

Something happened to this demonic man in the Mark 5 story that opened doors to the demons that possessed him. Maybe his parents treated him badly, so he had an attitude or a rebellious spirit. Maybe he was abused as a child. Whatever it was, it gave demons access to come inside him. He had unresolved issues which gave the demons legal access to his mind and body. He may have even been suffering from a spirit of rejection.

Demonic possession can take place in layers. Imagine a man who had a bad day at work, so he decides to visit a pub and drink a few beers. The devil convinces him to go to the pub more often to blow off some steam. Then he starts going home drunk. So he is now mad at the world, and drunk. He already thinks his boss doesn't like him and now his wife is nagging him about coming home drunk. Eventually, he starts hitting his wife and beating on the kids. He is taking out his anger and frustration on his family. Then Satan, the one who caused him to be where he is, comes and accuses him of being a bad husband and father. So, the man now has to deal with condemnation and guilt. He starts thinking, "Oh God, what did I do? I hit my wife. I hurt my kids. I'm no good."

The devil starts working on his mind. This man starts having thoughts like, "My wife doesn't like me. My kids don't like me. My boss doesn't like me." He starts going to the pub even more, drinking even more, taking out his anger and frustration even more and opens himself up to even more demons.

In Mark 5, we see this demon possessed man being put out of the town. He was living in the cemetery because nobody wanted this man around. He may have been causing too much trouble in town so he became an outcast. This didn't fix his problem, so he kept getting deeper and deeper in despair.

If Satan can get a little foothold in your life, he can destroy you. He just wants to get you to sin a little, compromise a little so you open a door to a small demon. It could just be a movie or music you should not watch or listen to. It could just be one scene in a movie. If you compromise a little, you could get a demonic spirit in you and that is just the beginning. It doesn't happen overnight. It starts little by little.

We need to have the Spirit of God in us so strong that we can see when it first starts. We should not have to wait to try solving the problem when the man is out in the tombs and he has tons of demons inside of him. When we see people just starting on drugs, we should have the power to set the captives free because Jesus gave us all power and all authority to do that and not wait until it gets really bad. When people come to church all the time and they are on fire for God, and suddenly we don't see them for a long time, we should go find out where they are. It doesn't take too much for somebody to backslide. They start out by missing a Sunday and then missing another Sunday. We need to be looking out for our brothers and sisters. We need to be our brother's keeper.

Never Lose Your Anointing

I knew a young man who was in Bible College when I was there. He was a wonderful and anointed young man in his late teen years. He usually sat beside me in class. He was so anointed, that when I started doing some miracle meetings in my building, I invited him to come and preach. He had an anointing like Smith Wigglesworth or A.A. Allen. He was powerfully anointed.

Satan will sometimes send people to block someone's ministries and that is what I believe happened to this young man. A girl showed up. She was a little bit older than he was, which I don't have a problem with. He asked me what I thought of the girl because he wanted to marry her. I said, "First of all, she has two babies. She's in her 20s. You're 18. I think you should wait. You're just barely graduating out of Bible College. You have your whole life in front of you."

He said, "I'm in love with her. Will you please take time to fast and pray, sister Joan, and tell me what you think."

I fasted and prayed. The young lady was a nice lady. I liked her. She was sweet, but something was not right. So I gave him my opinion. I said, "You know, I'm not telling you what you should do, but my opinion is, you need to slow it down."

Well, he didn't. He got married to her and the call of God on his life was so strong, he started a church. Within two years, she was off having affairs with some youths in his church and she was way older than those she was sleeping with. It destroyed his ministry. The anointing he had was not the same because he allowed the hurt, rejection and the thought that he was a failure consume him. But I believe God did not take away the anointing from him. The devil started working on his mind saying, "You don't have the anointing anymore because you messed up." I told him repeatedly that it was a lie. He still had the same anointing that was on him in Bible College. Yes, he made a mistake. He should have repented and moved forward. But we sometimes have to reach out and help other people. God truly restored the young man and he is strong in the Lord and is pastoring again.

Back to the demonic man in Mark 5. The people in the town didn't know what to do with him. He was somebody's son. He was not an animal. Maybe he had a wife and/or children, a mother or grandmother out there somewhere praying for him. So, here comes Jesus. There had to be at least 2,000 demons inside this man because Jesus cast the demons into the swine and the swine went over the hill and drowned. There were 2,000 pigs. We can't really know for sure how many demons there were because thousands of demons could have gone into each pig. The Bible says he had legions. Legions are like ten thousands of thousands of demons.

Satan attacked the boat Jesus was on, trying to stop Jesus from getting there because he knew the demonic possessed man was there and he didn't want Jesus to set the man free.

> **When he saw Jesus from afar, he ran and worshiped Him. And he cried out with a loud voice and said, "What have I to do with You, Jesus, Son of the Most High God? I implore You by God that You do not torment me." For He said to him, "Come out of the man, unclean spirit!" Then He asked him, "What is your name?" And he answered, saying, "My name is Legion; for we are many." Also he begged Him earnestly that He would not send them out of the country. Now a large herd of swine was feeding there near the mountains. So all the demons begged Him, saying, "Send us to the swine, that we may enter them." And at once Jesus gave them permission. Then the**

unclean spirits went out and entered the swine (there were about two thousand); and the herd ran violently down the steep place into the sea, and drowned in the sea. (Mark 5:6-13).

Demons do not worship God. People worship God. There was just enough of the man left that he fell down and worshiped Jesus. The devils had taken over the man's mind and body, but there was just enough in this man, a little glimpse of hope. Maybe he was thinking, "If I could just get to Jesus, maybe I could go back and live with my wife. If I could get back to Jesus, maybe I could get my job back. Maybe I can go back and live in town. Just maybe."

He saw Jesus and he ran to worship Jesus, but the devil took over and said, "What have I to do with You, Jesus, Son of the Most High God? I implore You by God that You do not torment me."

That man had lots of demons in him and Jesus told them to go into the swine. Demons are fallen angels and they are always looking for a host. They are looking for somewhere to live. They don't want to be out there in the abyss so they will always torment people trying to find out if they can open you up by watching pornography, lying, cheating, stealing, self-destruction or trying to get you oppressed. Demons will try to come inside of you so we need to stay prayed up. That is why Jesus said we must always be forgiving.

Don't leave any doorways open for demonic spirits to come into you.

> **Enter by the narrow gate; for wide is the gate and broad is the way that leads to destruction, and there are many who go in by it. Because narrow is the gate and difficult is the way which leads to life, and there are few who find it. (Matthew 7:13-14).**

Jesus is saying, "Narrow is the path that leads to heaven." There are things you used to do before becoming a Christian, that you will not want to do after you get saved. You will not want to watch certain movies, read certain books or listen to certain music anymore. The path gets narrower the longer you are a Christian. But broad is the road that leads to destruction and many there be that walk that road. We need to make ourselves available so we can help people when they are first starting to take that pill or when the oppression starts or when they first get sick.

So those who fed the swine fled, and they told it in the city and in the country. And they went out to see what it was that had happened. Then they came to Jesus, and saw the one who had been demon-possessed and had the legion, sitting and clothed and in his right mind. And they were afraid. (Mark 5:14-15).

Why were the townspeople afraid? They were not afraid when he was breaking chains. They were not afraid when he was causing all kinds of problems in town, but now that he was sitting there clothed and listening to Jesus, all of a sudden, the city was afraid and they asked Jesus to leave. How could they see a miracle before their own eyes, and tell the One who is the miracle worker, the One who set the man free from all those demons, to leave? The man was totally free and in his right mind and they asked Jesus to leave.

The man wanted to go with Jesus, but Jesus was smart. He said, "No. You can't go with me. Go back to town. Go back to your wife. Go back to your boss."

Can you imagine if that man had a wife and he went home and knocked on the door, the shock that would be on her face. I imagine he would say something like this, "Honey, I have seen the Lord. He has changed me. Please take me back in." He was a changed man. His children, if he had any, would hug him and say, "Our father was gone. Our father was lost. Our father was dead to us. Our father was mean but look. Look what the Lord has done." Jesus knew that his testimony would change the city. People would want to know, "Is that the same man who used to cause problems? What has happened to him?"

He would say, "Jesus set me free."

There are many people all around the world who were bound by devils and the Lord got a hold of them and turned them around. They became mighty men and women who are used powerfully by the hand of God to set people free because they knew what it was like to be bound. Now that they have found freedom, their desire is to see other people experience this freedom as well.

Let God's power change you so you can go and set the captives free.

Chapter 6
Faith To Free The Captives

And when He came to the disciples, He saw a great multitude around them, and scribes disputing with them. Immediately, when they saw Him, all the people were greatly amazed, and running to Him, greeted Him. And He asked the scribes, "What are you discussing with them?" Then one of the crowd answered and said, "Teacher, I brought You my son, who has a mute spirit. And wherever it seizes him, it throws him down; he foams at the mouth, gnashes his teeth, and becomes rigid. So I spoke to Your disciples, that they should cast it out, but they could not." He answered him and said, "O faithless generation, how long shall I be

with you? How long shall I bear with you? Bring him to Me." (Mark 9:14-19).

If Jesus referred to them then as a faithless generation, what would He call us today?

I tell you that He will avenge them speedily. Nevertheless, when the Son of Man comes, will He really find faith on the earth?" (Luke 18:8).

Will Jesus find us with great faith? Do we know that we have power and authority to command demons to come out of people, sickness to leave, cancer to be healed, blind eyes and deaf ears to be opened? Are we confident that we have the power in the name of Jesus to do the work that God has told us to do?

Then they brought him to Him. And when he saw Him, immediately the spirit convulsed him, and he fell on the ground and wallowed, foaming at the mouth. So He asked his father, "How long has this been happening to him?" And he said, "From childhood. And often he has thrown him both into the fire and into the water to destroy him. But if You can do anything, have compassion on us and help

us." Jesus said to him, "If you can believe, all things are possible to him who believes." Immediately the father of the child cried out and said with tears, "Lord, I believe; help my unbelief!" When Jesus saw that the people came running together, He rebuked the unclean spirit, saying to it, "Deaf and dumb spirit, I command you, come out of him and enter him no more!" Then the spirit cried out, convulsed him greatly, and came out of him. And he became as one dead, so that many said, "He is dead." But Jesus took him by the hand and lifted him up, and he arose. And when He had come into the house, His disciples asked Him privately, "Why could we not cast it out?" So He said to them, "This kind can come out by nothing but prayer and fasting." (Mark 9:20-29).

Normally when people see a child or anyone having a seizure, they would start to panic. But that is not what Jesus did. Jesus turned to the father of the child and had a conversation with him. Jesus wasn't too concerned because He knew He had the power.

We need to spend time in prayer because we don't know when God is going to use us. We don't know when there is going to be a car wreck and the Holy Spirit tells us to get out because someone is about to die and we need to raise them from the dead. It can happen at the most peculiar times.

God Will Use You Anywhere

When I first got saved, after about two years, some friends of mine made arrangements for me to be on TBN (Trinity Broadcasting Network) on the Praise the Lord Show. I had never been on TV before so I was really excited about being on television. I fasted for two or three days because I wanted to really be anointed.

The TBN set was designed in such a way that in between speakers, they would cut away to a song. So each speaker spoke for twenty minutes, then they would have a song while the other speaker is being brought on to the TV set stage. While they cut away to the song, there is enough time for them to prepare the other speaker with a microphone, make sure they are sitting properly and looking into the camera. When the song ends, the host comes on and introduces the next speaker.

I was sitting in the audience because I was the last speaker to go on. They had three segments. When it was my turn, they cut away to a song. I was given the necessary instructions about where I would walk to go up, etc. Before I got to the stage, a man came up to me and started attacking me. When I should be onstage getting ready for my segment, I was busy dealing with a demon that was manifesting. I was on the floor over this man's body saying, "Come out in the name of Jesus." I was supposed to be on the platform. I heard when the guy said, "Well, would Brother so and so come back on the set because Sister Joan is busy?" Others came to help me, and I didn't know how long it took, but the man was finally set free. I lead him to the Lord and to the baptism of the Holy Spirit, and he was on his merry way. By then, the cameras were off and I had missed my opportunity to be on TBN.

The devil had a plan to keep me from sharing my testimony all across the United States. So we need to always be ready to do spiritual warfare. Even though I had fasted and prayed, I didn't think something was going to come against me like that so I didn't pray that way. We need to know how to do warfare and stop things from coming.

Demons Can Physically Harm You

I was ordained under John G. Lake's Ministry. I was a part of that ministry fellowship and they had a conference every year with morning services and night meetings. I had a big house, so normally after the morning service, I would invite the ministers to come over to my house. There were about 30-40 ministers and their spouses. We would have a big feast with tables and chairs and everything needed to facilitate a big crowd.

Normally we would eat at about 1pm, and get ready to go back to the night service. It was about 1pm when I stepped into the kitchen to stir up some of the precooked food because it was warming up. I had an archway that led into the dining room area. All the pastors were in the dining room and living room area, walking back and forth. We were having a prayer meeting and they were praying in tongues. I walked from the kitchen into the room where they were, and suddenly something (a demon) hit me. It hit me so hard, it knocked all the air out of me, and I fell forward.

I was on the floor lying on my stomach and barely able to breathe. The pastors were walking around me, praying. I was trying to pray in the spirit but I couldn't talk. All I could do was think and pray silently. So, I thought, "Lord, please let these men know that I'm not laying here praying, that I am being attacked by a demon."

Suddenly, one of the pastors who did a lot of deliverance came over me and said, "Satan, you leave her alone now in the name of Jesus. I command you to come off her now. Come off of her now." I suddenly caught my breath.

A demon had hit me so hard that when I went to get ready for bed that night, there was a big black and blue mark where it hit me.

Lester Sumrall's Encounter

Lester Sumrall once had an encounter with a girl in the Philippines who was so demon-possessed that the demons would bite her and they would see teeth marks on her body. This is a true story. I preached in Lester Sumrall's church in the Philippines so I heard one of his testimonies of how the Lord blessed him with a building. He received it as a free gift. Lester Sumrall was a mighty man of God who knew how to do deliverance.

Nobody knew what to do about the young girl. Her parents would freak out when they saw the big teeth marks appearing on her body. The demons were biting her. So Lester Sumrall came and he cast a lot of demons out of the little girl and she was totally set free from all those demons. Her parents were rich, and the news about the little girl's deliverance went out all over Manila. It was broadcast in the newspapers and on TV and radio. The parents gave Lester Sumrall the building that I was priviledged to preach in. It was a big dome building on a whole city block. They gave it to him as a gift to start his church because he set their daughter free.

We have that power and God wants us to know that demons are real. God's power is much stronger than any demonic power. We have the power in the name of Jesus.

> **Then Jesus, being filled with the Holy Spirit, returned from the Jordan and was led by the Spirit into the wilderness, being tempted for forty days by the devil. And in those days He ate nothing, and afterward, when they had ended, He was hungry. (Luke 4:1-2).**

At the end of a forty day fast, Jesus was hungry. The devil will always attack us when we are weak. He will attack when we are exhausted; when we have not been in the word or praying; when we think we don't have to pray or go to church. The devil will wait until we are weak and then he attacks. So he waited until Jesus had been on the forty-day fast.

And the devil said to Him, "If You are the Son of God, command this stone to become bread." (Luke 4:3).

The devil knew that Jesus is the Son of God. So why did he use the word "if?" The word "if" is a doubt word. We need to get the word "if" out of our vocabulary. You don't need to be saying, "If this works, I could cast the devil out of this person." If you are not sure, you will not see it happen. We need to know who we are. We need to know that Christ is in us and we have all power and all authority because of the blood of Christ and because Jesus did it on the cross. When He said it was finished, that is what He meant. That means everything Jesus did, we can do. Jesus said we can do even greater things.

We are one with Jesus; one with the Father and one with the Holy Spirit. We can step out and start setting people free. What did Jesus say? Man shall not live by bread alone. We can use the Word of God against the devil. If the devil tries to put something on you, just start reading and quoting Scriptures. Tell the devil to shut up and tell him where to go. He has no right to talk to you.

Jesus cast demons out of people. He told His disciples, **"And as you go, preach, saying, 'The kingdom of heaven is at hand.' Heal the sick, cleanse the lepers, raise the dead, cast out demons. Freely you have received, freely give."** (Matthew 10:7-8).

Jesus Sent Out Seventy

Then the seventy returned with joy, saying, "Lord, even the demons are subject to us in Your name." And He said to them, "I saw Satan fall like lightning from heaven. Behold, I give you the authority to trample on serpents and scorpions, and over all the power of the enemy, and nothing shall by any means hurt you. Nevertheless do not rejoice in this, that the spirits are subject to you, but rather rejoice because your names are written in heaven." (Luke 10:17-20).

The minute we said, "Dear Jesus, come into my heart and be my Lord and Savior," we became a real Christian. Immediately, we can do the works that God has told us to do.

The Bible says Jesus rejoiced in the Spirit and said, "I thank You, Father, Lord of heaven and earth, that You have hidden these things from the wise and prudent and revealed them to babes. Even so, Father, for so it seemed good in Your sight."

Jesus had been trying to train His disciples to do the work that He told them to do. So, finally, the 70 came back and they were all probably talking at the same time. They were so excited and Jesus was happy. He basically said, "Oh, Father, I have been trying to train them for three years, and I was starting to wonder if they were ever going to get it, but I thank You, Father. They are getting it." We need to be God's hands and feet on the earth.

> **Then those who feared the Lord spoke to one another, and the Lord listened and heard them; so a book of remembrance was written before Him for those who fear the Lord and who meditate on His name. "They shall be Mine," says the Lord of hosts, "On the day that I make them My jewels. And I will spare them as a man spares his own son who serves him." Then you shall again discern between the righteous and the wicked, between one who serves God and one who does not serve Him. (Malachi 3:16-18).**

"For behold, the day is coming, burning like an oven, and all the proud, yes, all who do wickedly will be stubble. And the day which is coming shall burn them up," says the Lord of hosts, "That will leave them neither root nor branch. But to you who fear My name the Sun of Righteousness shall arise with healing in His wings; and you shall go out and grow fat like stall-fed calves. You shall trample the wicked, for they shall be ashes under the soles of your feet on the day that I do this," says the Lord of hosts. (Malachi 4:1-3).

Jesus sent twelve disciples and then He sent seventy disciples and now He is sending you. Go set the captives free.

Chapter 7
How The Devil Works

When the church rises up to the authority that God has given it, they will walk in the power and the anointing that God has placed on the body of Christ. God's Word says that we can do all things through Christ who strengthens us. We need to remember this. God said to His church:

> **Most assuredly, I say to you, he who believes in Me, the works that I do he will do also; and greater works than these he will do, because I go to My Father. And whatever you ask in My name, that I will do, that the Father may be glorified in the Son. If you ask anything in My name, I will do it. (John 14:12-14).**

In other words, we are to go in the power, might and authority of the Lord Jesus and do the same works He did. God said all we need to do is ask. We are not asking enough. God has given us power over demons, over all the demonic forces, and we need to reach out and touch the world.

We need to know how the devil works, so we can successfully help set the captives free.

> **But avoid foolish and ignorant disputes, knowing that they generate strife. And a servant of the Lord must not quarrel but be gentle to all, able to teach, patient, in humility correcting those who are in opposition, if God perhaps will grant them repentance, so that they may know the truth, and that they may come to their senses and escape the snare of the devil, having been taken captive by him to do his will. (2 Timothy 2:23-26).**

When people are doing drugs and drinking until their liver gets damaged, it is because they have been led captive by the demons to do their will. People don't realize that they open doors to the devil unless they come to their senses. Our country is in serious trouble right now because of addictions to pornography, drinking and marijuana. Legalizing marijuana is a doorway that made Satan very happy. It is a mind-changing drug, and that is what Satan wants. He wants the minds of our young people, the minds of our older people, and to see that they are literally out of their own senses. The devil has led them captive. People in their right minds don't do certain things. Those who are not in their right minds are those whose mind is controlled and altered by Satan's plans.

Let's see some of the other ways that the devil works. One other way that the devil works is through soul ties. The Bible says that when a husband and wife get married, they are one spirit. So someone who goes around having sex with multiple people will also inherit the demons those people carry because sex makes two people become one spirit. The connection that is made when people have sex is what is called soul ties, and you can have multiple soul ties to every single person you have sex with.

Many people make covenants and have soul ties to others, which leads to witchcraft. Let us go through some things that are hurting people. These are also ways that the devil will work.

But know this, that in the last days perilous times will come: For men will be lovers of themselves, lovers of money, boasters, proud, blasphemers, disobedient to parents,

111

unthankful, unholy, unloving, unforgiving, slanderers, without self-control, brutal, despisers of good, traitors, headstrong, haughty, lovers of pleasure rather than lovers of God, having a form of godliness but denying its power. And from such people turn away! For of this sort are those who creep into households and make captives of gullible women loaded down with sins, led away by various lusts, always learning and never able to come to the knowledge of the truth. (2 Timothy 3:1-7).

This Scripture sounds like it is describing people today. Even our children are disobedient and disrespectful to their parents. The Bible says that if you honor your mother and father, you will have a long life. Today, we have a lot of teenagers and young people dying early because they are not polite to their parents. They don't like their parents or the parents don't like them. There is a lot of anger going around. The devil can come through the doors of anger and strife.

We are admonished in Scripture to worship God with all our heart, might, soul and strength. But we have people who don't know Jesus who are worshiping money, fame and fortune. The Bible refers to some people as having a form of godliness but denying the power thereof. Let's talk about having a form of godliness. There are so many people who are "church-goers" only. They have a form of godliness but no power. It is just a ritual for them. We should go to church because we love God, not because we are going to get something out of it. Many people go to church because it is a family tradition to go. As soon as church is over, they leave and live like the devil. It is a form of godliness, not a lifestyle. Satan will take a lot of religious people to hell because they only have a form of godliness. They only appear to be godly, but they don't have a personal relationship with Jesus Christ. They have never asked Jesus into their heart and in some churches, they don't even do an altar call. They don't invite people to Christ and we have to wonder if some of these ministers in these churches have really accepted Jesus. We will talk more about wolves in sheep's clothing in the next chapter.

The Scripture says we should turn away from people who appear to be godly but they are not. If you are going to a church and you are not receiving anything; you are not being fed with the Word of God and there are no signs and miracles and Jesus is not setting captives free, you may want to consider going elsewhere. You should be able to go to a house of God and tell people your problems so they can do deliverance and help you to shut the door that was opened to Satan's schemes and plots.

> **I charge you therefore before God and the Lord Jesus Christ, who will judge the living and the dead at His appearing and His kingdom: Preach the word! Be ready in season and out of season. Convince, rebuke, exhort, with all longsuffering and teaching. For the time will come when they will not endure sound doctrine, but according to their own desires, because they have itching ears, they will heap up for themselves teachers; and they will turn their ears away from the truth, and be turned aside to fables. But you be watchful in all things, endure afflictions, do the work of an evangelist, fulfill your ministry. (2 Timothy 4:1-5).**

There are places and even churches that will lead people to hell.

Witch Doctor Gets Saved

I remember being asked to go to the Apache Indian tribe in Arizona. While I was there, we had a tent revival. It was an awesome tent revival and we had great and awesome miracles. In fact, we had so many miracles that I asked the pastor who was in charge if there was a witch doctor in town. He said, "Yes, there is a witch who does all kinds of witchcraft." I asked if I could go meet them and he asked, "Are you sure?"

I said, "Yeah, could you take me to their house?"

He took me to the house and they had some huge dogs in the yard. I wasn't afraid of demons but I did not like those big dogs. The dogs were not chained up so they were running around all over the yard. I allowed those I came with to go knock on the door so the owner could restrain the dogs so I could get in the house.

I took authority before I went in and bound up all the demonic spirits so I would have liberty in the Holy Spirit to speak. I shared the gospel with the witch doctor and his wife. His wife was in a wheelchair. Truly the Holy Spirit was using me on this encounter. We were there for about an hour and I think they must have liked me. I convinced them to come by the tent meeting.

115

They came out to the tent meeting on the last night. Amazingly, God healed the wife. She came out of the wheelchair. She started walking and the witch doctor then knew that our God was more powerful than his witchcraft. That night, both he and his wife accepted Jesus Christ as their Lord and Savior and were filled with the Holy Spirit.

The Chief Who Got Saved

One way that demons can get in is through bad doctrines. We must be careful of bad doctrines, other religions and cults as these are ways that demons can get into you. There are people who engage in worshiping devils, and Satanic worship and all kinds of occultic practices. They teach wrong doctrine. While I was on the Indian Reservation, they shared this story with me. The chief was the great grandfather of the pastor I was preaching for. When his grandfather was chief, they did not teach about Jesus because they wanted to do their own thing. But the chief was dying from cancer. They had a small hospital on the reservation. It was not a fancy hospital. The chief was admitted there dying and the doctors said he had cancer. They said, "You're dying of cancer. So get all your family together and say your goodbyes to them."

They called everybody in the tribe and the immediate family to come to the hospital. They came the next day to the hospital but in the middle of the night, the chief who was in the hospital had a dream. In the dream he was marching down a dirt road and everyone in the small reservation, maybe 300-400 people, were following behind him with their drums, etc. They were marching and doing their native dance. They came to a cliff and the chief stepped aside and watched as the entire tribe went over the cliff screaming as they fell off the cliff. He was seeing all this in a vision and he woke up screaming. Then he said Jesus appeared to him and asked him, "Why are you leading your people into what does not work?"

So the chief said to Jesus, "Who are you?"

Jesus said, "I am Jesus of Nazareth. You have taught them, trained them, and you are leading all your people into the pit of hell. Repent."

The chief was shaking and then Jesus said, "I'm going to prove to you that I am Jesus." Jesus touched him and said, "You are healed." The chief had the doctors test him and every bit of cancer was gone from his body and he did not die.

The chief called a tribal meeting and said to the gathering, "Is there anybody in this tribe who has a Bible?"

There was one young Native American boy in his twenties who had a Bible. He was reading the Bible and he had accepted Jesus, but he didn't want to tell anybody else on the reservation.

The chief asked again, "Anybody have a Bible? I really need somebody who has a Bible. It's very important because I need to tell you what Jesus did for me."

When the young man heard that, he thought it was safe, so he said, "I have a Bible."

The chief turned to the young man and said, "You're going to be the pastor. So from now on you need to read the Bible to us because I have to change what we're teaching."

Two generations later, I was there preaching and had the privilege to lead the tribal witch doctor and many of the American Indian people to the Lord. We had a great revival.

What is happening in other countries today is that people are having visions and dreams of Jesus because they are so rooted and grounded in bad teaching and bad doctrine that Jesus himself is appearing to them.

So, how do we escape the snares of the devil?

> **Therefore submit to God. Resist the devil and he will flee from you. Draw near to God and He will draw near to you. Cleanse your hands, you sinners; and purify your hearts, you double-minded. (James 4:7-8).**

God says we should come to the Lord. The devil can't stand it if we draw near to God; he will flee. If we humble ourselves under the mighty hands of God and put our trust in God, then God will set us free. Jesus is the one who will set you free.

> **Brethren, if anyone among you wanders from the truth, and someone turns him back, let him know that he who turns a sinner from the error of his way will save a soul from death and cover a multitude of sins. (James 5:19-20).**

> **There is therefore now no condemnation to those who are in Christ Jesus, who do not walk according to the flesh, but according to the Spirit. For the law of the Spirit of life in Christ Jesus has made me free from the law of**

119

sin and death. For what the law could not do in that it was weak through the flesh, God did by sending His own Son in the likeness of sinful flesh, on account of sin: He condemned sin in the flesh, that the righteous requirement of the law might be fulfilled in us who do not walk according to the flesh but according to the Spirit. For those who live according to the flesh set their minds on the things of the flesh, but those who live according to the Spirit, the things of the Spirit. For to be carnally minded is death, but to be spiritually minded is life and peace. Because the carnal mind is enmity against God; for it is not subject to the law of God, nor indeed can be. (Romans 8:1-7).

Jesus is saying we need to go talk to people. We should not wait until they are full of demons before we talk to them. There are different levels or categories of demonic oppression. The first stage, for example, is a little drugs or one drink in a pub. Eventually it is going to get worse. Satan first torments our minds with thoughts that lead to temptation. Then he will start piling on the heavier and stronger levels of oppression.

If we can minister to people at the beginning stages, setting them free will be so much easier.

The devil cannot enter anyone until he gets a legal right to do so, which is why he starts off small and works his way up until we are hooked or addicted. When we get to that stage, it is hard to get set free. We need to go to people at the starting point of their oppression, for example, talk to the people in bars, hanging out on the streets, etc. We need to make time to minister to people who are hurting so we can help to prevent doors being opened to the demonic.

Parents, we need to protect our children so be careful of the kind of books you buy because some of them are rooted in witchcraft. There are many demonic doors that are concealed in fiction so we must be careful. These kind of books are anti-God.

We must be careful of the movies we watch. The media is brainwashing our children through music, movies and books. We have the responsibility to protect our children and control what they are watching, listening to and reading. We need to be more careful with what comes into our homes.

Children Can Be Possessed Too

I have a long-time friend that I would go have a coffee with every now and then. She was an older lady, way older than me. She told me about her grandson who was about ten years old. She said he embarrasses her every time she takes him anywhere with her. So I asked her what was the problem.

She said, "Every time a pretty woman goes by, he slaps her on the rear and he goes 'hubba, hubba, hubba, hubba, hubba, oh.'" He has a problem with lust. He was always looking at women's body parts and talking about it.

I said, "That's not normal for someone so young."

She said, "Well can you spend some time with him? Something's not right and his parents are gone all the time and he's home by himself."

I eventually found out what it was. The parents had pornography videos in their bedroom and the little boy would watch these movies when his parents were gone. I had to spend some time with him and cast out the spirit of lust and other demonic spirits. Our children can also be demon possessed, so parents beware. I know of another case where a little boy about eight years old had demons that needed to be cast out. We need to protect our children from opening doors to demons so don't let them watch witchcraft and demonic type movies. We need to be able to discern the spirit that is behind the movies, music and books we allow our children to engage with.

Lucifer wants to brainwash our children so they will have homosexual thoughts, etc. There are even cartoons that are suggestive with transgenderism, homosexuality, etc. They are trying to convince us that these things are okay. We need to share the love of Jesus and be a witness to our children, but also warn them of the dangers of certain practices.

> **Therefore humble yourselves under the mighty hand of God, that He may exalt you in due time, casting all your care upon Him, for He cares for you. Be sober, be vigilant; because your adversary the devil walks about like a roaring lion, seeking whom he may devour. Resist him, steadfast in the faith, knowing that the same sufferings are experienced by your brotherhood in the world. (1 Peter 5:6-9).**

God is saying we need to resist the devil and tell him to get under our feet. We need to be vigilant in recognizing Satan when he comes with his subtle schemes. We need to pray and ask God to give us the gift of discerning of spirits so that we can recognize demonic spirits in what we bring into our houses, and the cartoons our children watch or anything that could open up a doorway in our homes and the lives of our families to demons. We need to resist the temptation to watch, read and listen to the wrong things. We don't need to be watching some of the garbage the enemy puts into our movies. We need to turn it off and watch and pray that our family members don't fall into the traps of the enemy.

Be a watchman over your family and protect them from what they are watching and reading.

Chapter 8
Wolves In Sheep's Clothing

For such are false apostles, deceitful workers, transforming themselves into apostles of Christ. And no wonder! For Satan himself transforms himself into an angel of light. (2 Corinthians 11:13-14).

Not everyone who says they are a prophet or apostle is who they say they are. We need to test the spirits to see what kind they are before we submit to a different teaching. There are false teachers who are teaching doctrines of demons. So we have to be careful what comes into our eyes and ears, and what we do with our body because that is how the devil works. Satan can disguise himself as an angel of light so he can deceive people. Here is an example. So many people think that because they have a dream that they are going to marry somebody. I can use a friend as an example. She got married and it was a disaster. I remember saying to her,

"How did you know you were supposed to marry him?" They knew each other practically all their lives. I said, "Did God say you were supposed to marry him?"

She said, "Oh, no. We were both out, sitting on a park bench and a rainbow came out and that was a sign from God that we should be married."

There was another person who said, "I always know that God is doing something great because when I see a butterfly flying and landing close to me, then I know 'oh that's God telling me something.'"

God is not in the butterfly and He is not a rainbow.

Another friend told me that whenever she sees a dove, it is a sign that she is supposed to do something. I would advise that we stay away from such crazy notions.

Meeting In India

I did a meeting in India a long time ago, and the pastors asked me to do a seminar as part of a group. They wanted me to teach pastors how to cast out devils. The pastor in charge of those meetings said there would be between a hundred and fifty and two hundred pastors. I said, "Sure, I'll do the best I can."

I was a baby Christian. Some of those pastors had been Christians for over 60 years. I thought, 'Who am I?' but the Lord said I should do it. So, I agreed to do the seminar.

On the day of the seminar, with about a hundred pairs of eyes looking at me, I said, "This is how you cast out devils. If a dog goes to attack me, and I see it growling and foaming at the mouth, I don't look at that dog and say, 'Nice dog,' because it's going to eat me up. Instead, I would say, 'Stop!' I must let that dog know that I have the authority and that I'm the alpha dog. That's how you handle demons. You say, 'Satan, come out in the name of Jesus!'"

I was demonstrating this point, and started shouting out loud, "Satan, come out in the name of Jesus." I was saying it continually. Suddenly, five pastors manifested demons all over the place. Demons were coming out of people everywhere and I hadn't even finished the seminar.

Suddenly, it became a practical seminar. I said, "All of you Pastors who are around a person that is manifesting demons, get over there and just start saying, "Come out, in the name of Jesus.""

127

There were five different people manifesting demons at the same time. I said, "This is a hands-on experience."

It took about forty-five minutes, and all who were possessed were set free. We need to know who we are in Christ Jesus and our authority as a believer. We need to stop walking in fear. The devils will know, just like the dog will know, if we are walking in fear.

Demons know if we have the authority, and if we are walking by faith in Jesus Christ and if we know the finished work of the cross of Calvary. Therefore, the devil knows that he must go because we have been given all power and authority over devils to put them under our feet. Because of Jesus, we have been given the power to tell the devils, "Get out, in Jesus' name."

Big Demon, Little Demon

When I came home from India, after three months, I was exhausted. It was a 25 hour flight back home. Usually those long flights will cause jet lag. It was 3 a.m. when I got home and I did not get any sleep on the plane. I may have dozed off a few times, but no real sleep so I was extremely exhausted. I was back in Kennewick, Washington and in my own bed so I quickly fell asleep. I was asleep for about an hour when my phone rang. I tried to ignore it, but it kept on ringing so I finally picked up the phone and answered. The lady on the phone said, "Oh, I'm so glad you're home. Pastor Doug told me you would be home today."

I said, "It's 3:00 in the morning. What's the problem?"

She said, "My son is trying to kill me. He's got demons in him."

I said, "Please call Pastor Doug and ask Pastor Doug to come over to your house."

She said, "Pastor Doug has been to my house and he tried doing the deliverance and nothing happened."

So I said, "Well, call Pastor John."

"Pastor John's been here too," She said.

"Well, call another pastor," I said, sounding quite annoyed.

"Oh, they've all been here and nothing happened. They said you know how to do deliverance."

I really didn't want to get out of bed and go. My body did not want to go. Suddenly, I heard screaming on the other end. She dropped the phone and I heard the phone hit the floor. She was screaming. She picked the phone back up and said, "My son's trying to kill me. He's got a knife. Hurry to my house." Her son was eight years old.

I knew where she lived, so I quickly drove over to her house. It wasn't a far drive. When I arrived, the son was chasing his mom around with a knife and making all kinds of growling noises. So I got a hold of him and did the deliverance and the demons started coming out. There was more than one demon. Sometimes when we get rid of one demon, we have to ensure that there are no others. The way the demons work is there are strong demons and other little demons. And sometimes the bigger demon will push one of the smaller ones out to distract the person doing deliverance and make them feel like the person is free. If the deliverance continues, the strong demon will push another smaller one out, but the big one will always remain. If all the smaller ones leave and the big one remains, he will just let all the others who were cast out back in.

While doing deliverance on the child, I noticed that a lot of the smaller demons left, but because I was operating in the gift of discernment, I knew the little boy was not free. I kept going until the big one came out and then the little boy was set free. I led him to the Lord and to the baptism of the Holy Spirit. Then, I decided to have a conversation with him. So I said, "Okay, I need to talk to you. So what have you been doing?"

What was an 8-year-old doing to open the door to so many demons?

He said, "Well, I didn't do anything."

I said, "Now, tell me what you do every day."

His mom told me that for the past three or four years he had been going out to his playhouse in the backyard. I asked them to show me, so they turned on the lights in the backyard and showed me the playhouse. I could see it, but it was still dark so I did not go out there. It was a nice little playhouse.

The little boy said that he had been talking to somebody out there for a couple years. He said a friend came to visit him. So someone was visiting him and spending time with him out there in his playhouse because he was lonely. When the devil saw that the little boy was lonely, he came as an angel of light to be the little boy's friend. The little boy had been communicating and fellowshiping with a demonic force for a couple of years, and the devil only became stronger. We need to be very careful of imposters who come as light, but they are really darkness. False prophets and false teachers are a real threat to those who believe in Jesus. If Satan can transform himself into an angel of light, it is expected that those who serve him can also transform themselves into ministers of righteousness whose end will be according to their works.

So there are false prophets and false teachers and most of them are self appointed. You can't call yourself into ministry. People assume titles that don't belong to them because they were not called of God.

> **For the weapons of our warfare are not carnal but mighty in God for pulling down strongholds, casting down arguments and every high thing that exalts itself against the knowledge of God, bringing every thought into captivity to the obedience of Christ, and being ready to punish all disobedience when your obedience is fulfilled. (2 Corinthians 10:4-6).**

We need to learn so we can teach and train others in the truth. If we are going to do deliverance, then we need to be able to identify when someone is having evil thoughts so we can bring those thoughts down. We can't stop the devil from throwing thoughts at us. Let's say, for example, you have a lustful thought. You need to know how to cast it down and not entertain it. Whether it is a thought to lie or steal, we need to be able to say, "No, Satan, those are not my thoughts." We need to take our thought life captive because that is where the devil targets. He targets our minds first in order to get to our will and emotions. That is how the devil works.

> **But if I cast out demons by the Spirit of God, surely the kingdom of God has come upon you. Or how can one enter a strong man's house and plunder his goods, unless he first binds the strong man? And then he will plunder his house. (Matthew 12:28-29).**

In a house occupied by demons, there is always a strong man. That is the demon I refer to as the big/strongest demon. He is responsible for bringing all the other little demons in. When we are doing deliverance, we need to make sure we are sensitive to the Holy Spirit and that we keep casting out the devils, including the strongest one, who is usually the last to go. If we leave the strong one in there, he is going to invite all the others to come back in. So we need to be careful of that.

133

When an unclean spirit goes out of a man, he goes through dry places, seeking rest, and finds none. Then he says, 'I will return to my house from which I came.' And when he comes, he finds it empty, swept, and put in order. Then he goes and takes with him seven other spirits more wicked than himself, and they enter and dwell there; and the last state of that man is worse than the first. So shall it also be with this wicked generation. (Matthew 12:43-45).

Our generation is getting more and more evil and we see it every day. When we do a deliverance and someone is delivered, we can't just leave them empty because the demons will come back and bring more with them. They will try to make sure no one can cast them out so easily the next time.

I have been to places where people love the thrill of going from church to church, causing distractions in the services. They would foam at the mouth and do all kinds of things just to get attention. They don't really want to be free, they are just seeking attention and they realize that they get it through the demons. So the demons keep coming back because the person enjoys the attention they get from causing distractions in the different churches.

When The Devil Comes To Kill The Evangelist

I was in Maine preaching in a Baptist Church. The pastor had called me and he said, "Sister Joan, we want to learn how to do evangelism, but we're not tongue talkers. So if you come to preach in my church, can you honor that? I don't want you doing any of that."

I said, "Yes, I can."

He said, "Now, I just want you to come and teach us how to do evangelism and that's it. You're going to be here three days and you can stay in the parsonage." The parsonage was across the street from the church.

On the second night of teaching, somewhere in the middle of my presentation, the back door flew open and a lady ran all the way up to the front. She grabbed me by the throat and she was choking me. The service was still going on, and there were people all over the place watching this woman choking me. I remembered what the pastor told me, but my life was at stake so I didn't have a choice but to start flowing in the gifts. So I said, "I command you, Satan, you come out." She fell to the floor foaming at the mouth and kicking. The people at

135

the seminar were petrified. While doing the deliverance, they all ran out of the church. At one point I looked up, and the church was empty. The people were gone. Only the pastor and his wife remained.

I stood over the lady commanding the demons to come out, and I heard the pastor's wife saying to her husband, "I told you these things are real. I saw this at Women's Aglow." Both of them eventually left, and I was alone with the woman in the church with no help from anybody. I kept on doing the deliverance, casting out demon after demon, until finally they were all gone. I then spent over an hour sharing Scriptures with her about salvation and the baptism of the Holy Spirit. She accepted Jesus and was filled with the Holy Spirit. She gave me her name and address so we could do follow up and disciple her and not leave her open for the demons to come back.

After it was all over, I figured I was in deep trouble. I was supposed to be there for three days and not flow in the gifts of the Spirit or speak in tongues. The lady left. She was now free, saved and filled with the Holy Spirit and I was walking across the street to the house. I knocked on the door. It was about midnight. I didn't realize I was at the church so long. The pastor and his wife were waiting up for me. He said, "We waited up for you."

I said, "Thank you, pastor."

He said, "Have a seat, young lady."

My immediate thought was, "Oh my God. I am in trouble." I was not supposed to be talking about the Holy Spirit and I ended up doing a full deliverance causing the whole church to disappear.

The pastor said, "I want you to know something, Sister Joan, we have been a traditional Baptist Church for 150 years, and we have never in the 150 years seen anything like what happened tonight in our church service."

I was waiting for them to tell me to pack up and leave.

He continued, "I just want to know one thing, how do I get the power to do what you did?"

In shock, I said, "Well, Pastor, you remember that subject you told me I couldn't talk about?"

He asked, "You mean, the Baptism of the Holy Spirit and all that?"

I said, "Yep, Jesus said you shall receive power when the Holy Ghost has come upon you to do the work that God's called you to do. So if you want that power, then I have to explain to you how to receive the infilling of the Holy Spirit."

He and his wife said, "We want it. We're not going to bed until we get it."

It was about 1 a.m. and I started to do a whole Bible study on the Holy Spirit with that couple. They had such bad teaching against it and I needed to undo that before we could proceed. I wanted them to understand the importance of being filled with the Holy Spirit. I taught them for about an hour and they both just started speaking in tongues. I did not get kicked out of the church. I was allowed to finish the rest of the week. We never know how God is going to use us.

I found out that the lady who came in and tried to choke me had been to many other churches. She had also been delivered at those churches. I spoke to some of the pastors who knew her. She went from church to church and everybody was doing deliverance on her but it seems they would only cast out one or two of the little demons. The bigger ones kept coming back and bringing more. So every time she went to a church and two or three of the demons were cast out, seven more came in. Then she went to another church growling and making noise and a few more were cast out, and more came in. So she kept getting worse until that day when she tried to kill me. The demon in her was using her to try and kill me.

We need to know how to shut the door to demons when we do deliverance. We can't just leave them open. We need to disciple those who receive deliverance and be a friend to them. We need to get them a Bible, invite them to church and help to renew their minds so they can be strengthened in the things of God. God wants us to do that.

Satan Worshipers In Columbia Park

I was doing a meeting in a church in Kennewick, Washington, and then we went out to do an outreach in Columbia Park. We were doing street evangelism so we were walking up to people, handing them tracts and talking to them about Jesus. I saw two teenagers talking to each other. I walked up to the two teenagers and started sharing with them the love of Jesus.

Demons hate the word "Jesus." If you are in a church service and you see someone who is agitated, it is usually a demon in them. They can't rest because they don't like being around praise music and hearing people talk about Jesus. In that kind of atmosphere, the Holy Spirit is irritating the demon in them.

So I walked up to the two boys and I said, "You guys need Jesus." Immediately, one of the boys took off screaming. He seemed to have lost his mind. He started screaming and flashing his hands all over and took off running through the park like a crazy person. I ran after him because I felt like I needed to help that boy. So I was running after him but he was running faster than me. I couldn't catch up with him so I gave up and went back to the other boy. I said to him, "I'm really sorry about your friend. I don't know what got into him. I just said 'Jesus.'"

He said, "Oh, that's probably what happened. It was because you said Jesus."

I wanted to know what he was talking about. So he continued, "Well, we're both Satan worshippers."

I asked, "You worship Satan?"

He said, "Well, I don't know if I want to worship Satan anymore, but we are both Satan worshipers. At his house he has his bedroom on the top floor and we do seances all the time and call demons to come to see us. We also do sacrifices for Satan."

I was curious, "Are you kidding me?"

He said, "No. We've been into a lot of really bad things, but it's scaring me because strange things are happening to me, and I'm having terrible dreams. The more we do this satanic stuff, the more scared I'm getting. So I don't know what got into me. I went down to the Bible bookstore and said if the devil is real, then God must be real and I need to find an answer. I went and bought a Bible. I read the end of the Bible and according to the Bible I'm on the wrong side because Satan and the false prophets are going to be thrown in the lake of fire, and I'm thinking 'Oh, man, I need to switch sides. I don't need to worship Satan. I've got to find out how to worship God, but I don't know how."

I told him I knew how, and he said, "Well, I've been looking for somebody to find out how to get saved and delivered because I need to tell my friend. We need to get out of this Satan thing. It's getting really scary."

So, I led him to the Lord and he received Jesus as his Lord and Savior and he started attending church. I asked him for his friend's number and he gave me his number and the number for his parents. He didn't want to at first, but he finally did. I told him I would get help for his friend.

I called the number and no one answered. I left several messages introducing myself and asking him to call me back. I left messages for his parents. I left a voicemail that said, "Please, call me back. My name is Joan Pearce. I am a minister and I really need to talk to you about your son because it's very serious what's going on with your son." I left a lot of messages.

Finally, after a few days, his mother answered the phone and said, "We'd appreciate it if you'd stop calling. We don't want your ministry to help my son. I don't know what happened to him. He went to the park last Saturday, and he had a nervous breakdown and he's in the mental hospital."

So I said, "I didn't know he'd been in the mental hospital. Did you know that your son is doing Satanic rituals upstairs in his bedroom?"

She said firmly, "Just leave me alone lady. It's just kid's stuff. It's him and his friend up there doing stuff. Lighting candles and doing stuff. Just leave us alone and don't you call back again or I'll call the police."

I didn't get a chance to tell her that he snapped when I said "Jesus." The demon in the boy recognized that I was trying to witness to him. His friend was saved and already trying to read the Bible which would have influenced him, so the devil thought, "I need to take him out now." He lost his mind and ended up in the mental ward.

What they were practicing was not kid's stuff. Chanting, worshiping Satan and lighting candles is harmful and dangerous for children and adults. No child or adult should be involved in such things because it opens a door to Satan. We have the power to set the captives free but we need to be able to recognize how people get where they are and how we are going to set them free.

The Man In The Park

Columbia Park is a big park in Kennewick, Washington where we lived, so I liked to go for walks there very early in the morning. One morning, I went for a walk. This was a year or two after the encounter with those two young Satan worshippers. I was walking by the pond when I heard the Holy Spirit say to me, "In a few minutes, there's going to be a man walking on the same path as you. When he comes to you, he's going to turn around and walk with you."

143

So, I turned around and sure enough there was a man walking towards me. When he gets to me, just like the Holy Spirit, He said, "Hi, lady. How are you doing? Do you care if I walk with you?"

The Holy Spirit immediately sounded an alarm. He said, "He's going to hurt you."

The man was walking with me and we were walking to where my car was parked close to the Columbia River. The river had an embankment so when the flood waters get too high, it would go over the ledge. If you went over the embankment, you would go down into a little ravine and the other people in the park could not see you. But there was nobody else in the park. I looked around after the Holy Spirit told me this man would hurt me. We were the only ones there.

When we reached the river, he said, "Why don't we just go down to this ravine?"

I knew I didn't want to go there with him because if I did, nobody could see, even though no one was there, and he could do whatever he wanted to me and nobody would hear me calling for help. So I said, "No, I have to get something out of my car. So, let me go get something." God was giving me wisdom. I made him think that I needed to go to my car. When we reached my car, I started to unlock the door and he pinned me with his body. He was all over me, trying to take advantage of me sexually. Suddenly, I said with all the authority I had, "Satan, I command you, spirit of lust, to come off this man right now in the name of Jesus Christ. You spirit of lust come off him now!"

The man came to his senses immediately. He said, "Who are you? What am I doing here?"

I told him, "Nothing. You were walking me to my car."

I had no intention of staying in that park and doing deliverance on that guy. I planned to get out of there asap.

He said, "I was walking you to the car? Who are you?"

I said, "Never mind. You were just a nice gentleman and you're walking me to the car. Thank you very much."

I got in the car, started the engine, locked the door and I was out of there.

The man didn't know what he was doing because the spirit was controlling him. When I commanded the spirit of lust to leave him, he snapped back to himself. That is the power we have.

We need to renew our minds so we know and operate in who we are. When we deliver people from demons, it is very important that we teach them how to be saved and help them be filled with the Holy Spirit. We don't just do deliverance, but we should help those who are set free from demonic oppression so they stay free.

I beseech you therefore, brethren, by the mercies of God, that you present your bodies a living sacrifice, holy, acceptable to God, which is your reasonable service. And do not be conformed to this world, but be transformed by the renewing of your mind, that you may prove what is that good and acceptable and perfect will of God. (Romans 12:1-2).

When our minds are renewed, and we do deliverance, we are able to help those who are set free from demons to renew their minds as well. We must stay in the Word of God. As we study His Word on how to do deliverance and keep practicing, the Word will get in us and God will use us to do great and mighty things.

May God use you for His glory, in Jesus Name.

Chapter 9
Freely You Have Received, Freely Give

There are so many people all throughout the earth who are bound by demonic spirits. We need to learn how to pray for people and set them free from demons.

> **And as you go, preach, saying, 'The kingdom of heaven is at hand.' Heal the sick, cleanse the lepers, raise the dead, cast out demons. Freely you have received, freely give. (Matthew 10:7-8).**

We have received so much from Jesus. He has given us all power and all dominion so we can go out and see people healed, delivered, and cast demons and oppressing spirits out of people.

> **And when they had come to the multitude, a man came to Him, kneeling down to Him and**

saying, "Lord, have mercy on my son, for he is an epileptic and suffers severely; for he often falls into the fire and often into the water. So I brought him to Your disciples, but they could not cure him." Then Jesus answered and said, "O faithless and perverse generation, how long shall I be with you? How long shall I bear with you? Bring him here to Me." And Jesus rebuked the demon, and it came out of him; and the child was cured from that very hour. Then the disciples came to Jesus privately and said, "Why could we not cast it out?" So Jesus said to them, "Because of your unbelief; for assuredly, I say to you, if you have faith as a mustard seed, you will say to this mountain, 'Move from here to there,' and it will move; and nothing will be impossible for you. However, this kind does not go out except by prayer and fasting." (Matthew 17:14-21).

If we study the life of the early church, they fasted quite often. Most of the early church fasted at least a day or two per week. They lived a life of fasting. God wants us to know that some demons are so big that we need to fast. We don't fast to make the demons go out but we fast so that we are filled with the power and the glory of God. If we live a life of fasting, stay in prayer and seek God diligently, the stronger our faith in God will become and we will see a greater glory and manifestations flowing through us. We will see God's miracle working hands.

We need to mix faith with the Word of God. Jesus Christ has already paid the price. He spoiled principalities. He took the keys of death and hell from Satan. When He said "It is finished" on the cross, He had already done everything that He needed to do. Then He turned to us and said, "It's your turn to go." We cannot walk in fear. We must walk in faith.

My First Deliverance

About one year after accepting Jesus as my Lord and Savior, I started out in ministry by having a Bible study at my house. I didn't know how to read when I first started doing the Bible study. I was totally illiterate, but John G. Lake's daughter and son-in-law started coming to my Bible study because they lived in my neighborhood. They laid hands on me and declared that God would supernaturally teach me to read. Within a day or two, I was reading. I wasn't perfect but I was reading. God told me that if I read the Bible from

151

Genesis to Revelation, He would put me in full-time ministry in one year.

It was wonderful having the support of John G. Lake's daughter and son-in-law. They helped me by calling some of their pastor friends to get me started. While I was doing the Bible study in my house, I was still a fairly new Christian and after God taught me to read, I decided that I didn't really know a lot about demons. So I decided to get one of Lester Sumrall's books on demons because he was an expert on demons. I bought one of his workbooks and every week we would go through his workbook. I could read so it was a very simple book to read.

One day, after the Bible study, everybody left, except my friend, Mary Lou, and a lady who had been a guest that day. It was a Friday morning. Because we had been talking about demons so much, the lady had some concerns, so she initiated a conversation while I was making a cup of tea. She said, "I have these spirits that torment me all the time and there are voices that talk to me all the time."

Lester Sumrall's book says we must yell at demons and tell them to come out but what did I know? I was a fairly new Christian. That was my first time doing deliverance. So I said, "Well, let me just pray for you." I stood over the lady and I started saying, "Come out in the name of Jesus. I command you, Satan, to come out."

I was in for a surprise because those demons started coming out. I saw things that were not normal. No human can do what that lady did. Her head spun all the way around. She dropped to the floor and a different voice came out of her. She was slithering all over the living room floor like a snake and making all kinds of noises. A man's voice was coming out of the woman. Mary Lou was afraid. I told her to pray. Instead, she was busy running from the lady. The demon recognized Mary Lou's fear and went after her. So I had a friend consumed by the spirit of fear and a demon-possessed lady in my house.

I realized that Mary Lou had no faith, so I told her, "Go in the other room or go home or something. Just go somewhere. Go in the other room and pray." Her unbelief was causing the demon to act up.

We need to walk by faith when doing deliverance and don't keep people around who are not in agreement. For four or five hours I was casting one demon out after another. Each one was stronger than the one before. The strongman just kept pushing out all the smaller

153

demons and I kept casting them out. I had no human help because Mary Lou was afraid. But I had the Father, Son and Holy Spirit with me. I kept commanding the demons to leave and they became stronger and stronger. I realized that it was getting very powerful. All the little ones were gone and I was getting down to the big one. Layer upon layer the demons came out but it was too much. So I called my pastor and said, "Pastor, hurry and come to my house. I'm doing a deliverance."

He laughed and said, "Oh, Sister Joan, what are you into now?" Suddenly, the demon lady came screaming at me in another voice, cursing. Pastor asked with alarm in his voice, "What is that?"

I said, "I told you. It's a demon."

Within a few minutes, my pastor showed up. We both prayed. Together we continued with the deliverance. By that time, the demonic manifestation had become even more powerful. This is because we had reached the place where we had uncovered the main demon that was controlling the person and, of course, it did not want to come out. It was at that point where I understood why Jesus told demons to be quiet and not speak. This demon in the lady said, "It's my blood. I'm the one that paid the price for everybody. It's my blood that sets people free."

I was upset that the demon thought it was his blood. I told it to, "Shut up." The strongman in that lady was the spirit of lust. She started to slither her body all over my pastor's body. I thought, "Oh, my God." We both ganged up on the demon that was in her. When that last demon came out, she was limp from exhaustion.

We have the power to tell demons where to go and we don't need to know their names. I know there are people writing manuals on demons and giving them names, but our duty is to cast them out. We don't need to know their names. They are liars anyway, so we need to trust the Holy Spirit to tell us what the spirit is. I have done so many deliverances in different countries that now I just tell the demons to come out. I don't want to have a conversation with the devil. Jesus didn't let them talk. You have the power to set the captives free through the blood of the cross of Calvary, and we need to step into that.

Assuredly, I say to you, whatever you bind on earth will be bound in heaven, and whatever you loose on earth will be loosed in heaven. Again I say to you that if two of you agree on

earth concerning anything that they ask, it will be done for them by My Father in heaven. For where two or three are gathered together in My name, I am there in the midst of them. (Matthew 18:18-20).

When two or three are gathered together, Jesus is there. It is not us doing the deliverance, but the power of Jesus that is present where there is faith in Him. The presence of God will manifest where there is faith in the finished work of Christ to set people free. Remember to walk by faith, not fear.

Therefore I remind you to stir up the gift of God which is in you through the laying on of my hands. For God has not given us a spirit of fear, but of power and of love and of a sound mind. (2 Timothy 1:6-7).

God has blessed and equipped us to do the work He has called us to do.

Blessed be the God and Father of our Lord Jesus Christ, who has blessed us with every spiritual blessing in the heavenly places in Christ, just as He chose us in Him before the foundation of the world, that we should be

holy and without blame before Him in love, having predestined us to adoption as sons by Jesus Christ to Himself, according to the good pleasure of His will, to the praise of the glory of His grace, by which He made us accepted in the Beloved. In Him we have redemption through His blood, the forgiveness of sins, according to the riches of His grace which He made to abound toward us in all wisdom and prudence, having made known to us the mystery of His will, according to His good pleasure which He purposed in Himself, that in the dispensation of the fullness of the times He might gather together in one all things in Christ, both which are in heaven and which are on earth—in Him. In Him also we have obtained an inheritance, being predestined according to the purpose of Him who works all things according to the counsel of His will, that we who first trusted in Christ should be to the praise of His glory. In Him you also trusted, after you heard the word of truth, the gospel of your salvation; in whom also, having believed, you were sealed with the Holy Spirit of promise, who is the guarantee of our inheritance until the redemption of the purchased possession, to the praise of His glory. (Ephesians 1:3-14).

Jesus has blessed you with spiritual blessings and faith, so step out and set the captives free.

Chapter 10
Greater Works

John 14:12 says:

> Most assuredly, I say to you, he who believes in Me, the works that I do he will do also; and greater works than these he will do, because I go to My Father.

But what are the "greater works?"

> Then they went into Capernaum, and immediately on the Sabbath He entered the synagogue and taught. And they were astonished at His teaching, for He taught them as one having authority, and not as the scribes. Now there was a man in their synagogue with an unclean spirit. And he cried out, saying, "Let us alone! What have we to do with You, Jesus of Nazareth? Did You come to

destroy us? I know who You are—the Holy One of God!" But Jesus rebuked him, saying, "Be quiet, and come out of him!" And when the unclean spirit had convulsed him and cried out with a loud voice, he came out of him. Then they were all amazed, so that they questioned among themselves, saying, "What is this? What new doctrine is this? For with authority He commands even the unclean spirits, and they obey Him." And immediately His fame spread throughout all the region around Galilee. (Mark 1:21-28).

If you start having great success through God in deliverance, people will be coming to you from all over. They will hear that you know how to set people free, even though it is Jesus doing it, and they will find you.

At evening, when the sun had set, they brought to Him all who were sick and those who were demon-possessed. And the whole city was gathered together at the door. Then He healed many who were sick with various diseases, and cast out many demons; and He

did not allow the demons to speak, because they knew Him. (Mark 1:32-34).

Again, we see that Jesus is not talking to the demons, He just takes care of business. When we are doing deliverance, we need to focus on just casting out the demons. If they try to speak, we have the authority to shut them up. You have all power.

Then they brought to Him one who was deaf and had an impediment in his speech, and they begged Him to put His hand on him. And He took him aside from the multitude, and put His fingers in his ears, and He spat and touched his tongue. Then, looking up to heaven, He sighed, and said to him, "Ephphatha," that is, "Be opened." Immediately his ears were opened, and the impediment of his tongue was loosed, and he spoke plainly. (Mark 7:32-35).

Most sickness is from demons. If we cast the demon out, the sickness will go. We can speak to the spirit behind the sickness to bring healing to someone who is sick. We can speak to cancer and tell it to shrivel up and dissipate. We can speak to the spirit of deafness and command it to leave. God gave us the power through the name of Jesus Christ to do that. God says whatever we ask for in prayer in His Name, He will do it that He may be glorified.

God has granted you the power to cast out demons. So, how many devils have you ever cast out? Have you ever attempted to deliver anyone from demonic oppression or do you just watch people suffer feeling helpless? There are many people even around you who need deliverance. If God has equipped you to do it and you don't, what do you think is going to happen to them? When we see people suffering, we should not be afraid to walk up to them and say, "Let me pray for you. Satan I bind this sickness" or take authority over whatever is holding them back and loose them in Jesus' name. We need to bind devils and loose people into God's hands. We have that power.

And He said to them, "Go into all the world and preach the gospel to every creature. He who believes and is baptized will be saved; but he who does not believe will be condemned. And these signs will follow those who believe: In My name they will cast out demons; they will speak with new tongues; they will take up serpents; and if they drink anything deadly, it will by no means hurt

162

them; they will lay hands on the sick, and they will recover." So then, after the Lord had spoken to them, He was received up into heaven, and sat down at the right hand of God. And they went out and preached everywhere, the Lord working with them and confirming the word through the accompanying signs. Amen. (Mark 16:15-20).

God says if we lay hands on the sick, they will recover. We have more power than we can ever imagine. We have power over witchcraft.

Jealous Witch

I was in Alaska and I was with two pastors and we were sitting and talking about setting up a school of ministry that we were going to do in Alaska. Suddenly, I felt something stabbing me in the heart. I was still single at that time, and one of the pastors was also single.

There was a lady in the church who believed that the single pastor was supposed to be her husband. So whenever I went to minister at that church, she must have thought that I was a threat. We were pretty much the same age and we all went to Bible College together, so we were friends.

When I felt the stabbing in my heart, I didn't know what was going on. I just knew I was getting stabbed right in my heart. The pastors, thank God, were smart and in tune with the Holy Ghost. So they started praying, "We reverse whatever curse is on Joan. We reverse this curse." I don't think we should pray that way, but they did. The pain left within seconds, and then the phone rang. The young lady who expressed an interest in the pastor was in the hospital. They were suspecting a heart attack. She was in the hospital for over three hours. They ran tests and said she did not have a heart attack. We found out later that she had a voodoo doll that she named "Joan" and she was stabbing the doll and I was feeling it in my heart. When the pastors prayed, it reversed and went back to her.

I don't think we need to reverse anything. We should send it to the pit of hell and not put it back on people. My recommendation is that we don't go reversing curses. If we do, we are also dealing in witchcraft ourselves. We don't reverse curses; we break curses. Jesus became a curse to redeem us from all curses so we have the power to break curses. When you break the curse, don't put it back on the person. Send it into the abyss.

And from the days of John the Baptist until now the kingdom of heaven suffers violence, and the violent take it by force. (Matthew 11:12).

We are in a battle, so make sure you wear your armor.

Finally, my brethren, be strong in the Lord and in the power of His might. Put on the whole armor of God, that you may be able to stand against the wiles of the devil. For we do not wrestle against flesh and blood, but against principalities, against powers, against the rulers of the darkness of this age, against spiritual hosts of wickedness in the heavenly places. Therefore take up the whole armor of God, that you may be able to withstand in the evil day, and having done all, to stand. Stand therefore, having girded your waist with truth, having put on the breastplate of righteousness, and having shod your feet with the preparation of the gospel of peace; above all, taking the shield of faith with which you will be able to quench all the fiery darts of the wicked one. And take the helmet of salvation, and the sword of the Spirit, which is the word of God; praying

165

always with all prayer and supplication in the Spirit, being watchful to this end with all perseverance and supplication for all the saints. (Ephesians 6:10-18).

The Witch That Switched

I was in Pennsylvania a few years ago and there was a pastor where I went to preach who came to me and said, "Sister Joan, we're so glad you're here because we made an appointment for you to go meet the witch in town." There was no notice and he didn't ask me before if I wanted to take one of my afternoons to go see the witch in town. He just made the appointment. He said, "This lady is a practicing witch and she always calls when we run an ad in the paper. We always run an ad in the paper when we have a guest speaker. So she doesn't know you but believe me, she has had several of my speakers set an appointment so she said she wants you to come to her house." So I went to her house.

I thought the pastor was going to stay with me as backup support and because I didn't have a car but he didn't. He dropped me off and said, "I'll pick you up in a few hours."

I thought, "Well, thank you, pastor. This is really sweet of you."

The lady met me at the door and I went into the house and it was totally dark. She had blackout drapes over all the windows. There were lit candles throughout the house with some burning incense. I could hear some strange demonic type music playing in the background and she had black cats all over the place. We had to be pushing cats out of the way. It felt like a real scene from a movie at a witch's house.

She took me through the house and there were demonic symbols all over. She took me to the kitchen, which was also dark, and she said, "Have a seat. Can I fix you a cup of coffee?"

I thought to myself, "I don't want to drink or eat anything here." So I kindly said to her, "No, thank you."

So she sat down, then said, "I know you're a minister but I want to ask you a question. I hate my mother-in-law, and I took a voodoo doll and I stabbed it repeatedly while saying, 'Die mother-in-law.' She ended up in the hospital and she died of a heart attack. So I want to ask you, 'Did I kill her?'"

I said, "Yes, you did. Now, listen to me very carefully. Life and death are in the power of the tongue and when you do things like that, you release demons on assignment, just like angels can go on assignments. Even if you talk bad of people, they can sometimes feel a heaviness in the spirit realm that comes on them because you have been speaking against them. That is why even gossiping is bad because we loose spirits on people that torment them. Words are powerful."

She said, "So you really think I killed her?"

"Yeah, but there's hope for you. God forgives murderers so you can come to Jesus, and He will forgive you for killing your mother-in-law."

She got up and blew out all her candles and turned the lights on. Then she said, "You know what, I'm going to listen to you lady because you're the first evangelist or person to come here and not judge me. Every time I see an ad in the paper, I call the pastor and ask if they can send the evangelist or prophet or whatever to my house. As soon as they get in, they start judging me. 'You shouldn't have skeletons. You shouldn't have this. You shouldn't have that kind of music.' By the time they get to the kitchen, they've already judged me. You haven't said a word about anything. So, I'm going to listen to what you have to say."

I shared with her for about an hour and she accepted Jesus. Her son came home shortly afterwards. I told him that his mom just switched and she was not a witch anymore. I showed her Scripture after Scripture how witchcraft was not right and she denounced all of it. In order to get a witch, Mormon, fortune-teller, etc. saved, they have to first denounce their former practices. The son was happy that she accepted Jesus. He said, "I am so happy. I know my mom's been doing this and it really has been bothering me."

I set my mind on going home when, suddenly, the doorbell rang. It was a Jehovah's Witness. The boy said, "I'm studying with the Jehovah's Witness. It's time for me to have my lesson." I guess it wasn't time for me to leave yet. I sat with them for about forty five minutes. Everything the Jehovah's Witness said, I had a Scripture against it, until finally the Jehovah's Witness was so upset that he got up and left.

The son said to me, "You know what, you have been sent here by God. I have been studying for several months with that Jehovah's Witness and I didn't have a good feeling that it was the right thing for me to be studying.

So I asked God that if this is an error and I was not supposed to be a Jehovah's Witness, please let someone come to my house who knows Scriptures and could show me through the Holy Word that it's wrong. You have cleared my mind today."

That boy was only thirteen years old. I turned to him and asked, "So do you want to ask Jesus in your heart just like your mom did an hour ago?"

He said yes. They both got saved and I told them not to let that Jehovah's Witness come back again.

We have power over curses and all voodoo and every kind of witcraft.

> Now He was teaching in one of the synagogues on the Sabbath. And behold, there was a woman who had a spirit of infirmity eighteen years, and was bent over and could in no way raise herself up. But when Jesus saw her, He called her to Him and said to her, "Woman, you are loosed from your infirmity." And He laid His hands on her, and immediately she was made straight, and glorified God. But the ruler of the synagogue answered with indignation, because Jesus

170

had healed on the Sabbath; and he said to the crowd, "There are six days on which men ought to work; therefore come and be healed on them, and not on the Sabbath day." The Lord then answered him and said, "Hypocrite! Does not each one of you on the Sabbath loose his ox or donkey from the stall, and lead it away to water it? So ought not this woman, being a daughter of Abraham, whom Satan has bound—think of it—for eighteen years, be loosed from this bond on the Sabbath?" And when He said these things, all His adversaries were put to shame; and all the multitude rejoiced for all the glorious things that were done by Him. (Luke 13:10-17).

Demons can actually suppress people. This lady was bent over for many years. She had a demon on her back, pushing her over. As soon as Jesus told that demon to jump off her back, she straightened up and she was set free.

Take Charge Of Your Thoughts

A very strange thing happened while we were in India on one of our missions trip. We had about 5,000 people come to our meeting for prayer. There were four or five ministers praying and we each had our own prayer line. Everybody was coming up for prayer. We were praying for people for over five hours.

I was working with an interpreter when, suddenly, my interpreter was nowhere to be found. I could no longer ask people what they wanted prayer for so I just laid hands on them and prayed. It would take all night anyway if I had to ask each person what they needed prayer for.

A lady came up and she was bent over. She had a huge lump on her back and she could hardly walk. I am not so sure what happened, but I was in the spirit and I punched her with everything I had. I hit her in the back, and in the forehead at the same time. She was about 90 years old. When I hit her, she straightened up immediately.

The devil tried to put all kinds of crazy thoughts in my head to question why I punched her in two places. I was looking around to make sure other people weren't staring at me because I was on a missions trip with a whole bunch of people. My pastor was also there. I thought to myself, "I hope nobody saw me do that because they are going to tell me to go home." The devil was bombarding my mind with negative thoughts,

"Nothing happened. You don't have faith. You don't have faith."

Casting down arguments and every high thing that exalts itself against the knowledge of God, bringing every thought into captivity to the obedience of Christ. (2 Corinthians 10:5)

We must learn to cast down the enemy's thoughts. I was having a lot of negative thoughts because I had never punched anyone before. I even thought that maybe she was pretending to be sick because she stood up straight immediately after I punched her.

The next night, they had testimony time. During the testimony time, she got up and testified. The lady was yelling something in her language and looking at me. I thought for sure that she was telling the people that I punched her and that they should take me off the mission's team. I turned to the interpreter to find out what she was saying. I was extremely nervous. The interpreter says, "Wow, Sister Joan. She is saying she had been bent over like that for 27 years and you prayed for her last night and she was healed."

I thought, "She thinks I prayed for her? She doesn't realize I punched her?"

Everyone was applauding. I turned to the interpreter and asked, "Did she say anything else?"

He said, "Nope."

She didn't remember or didn't realize that I had punched her. She never said a word about that.

I decided that I must have slugged the demon and not the woman. In that case, I didn't have to tell the demon to come out. It was the anointing that broke the yoke of her sickness. I usually pray for hours before a meeting. Can you imagine the anointing after praying for three or four hours? The anointing gets stronger with fervent prayer. I believe the anointing was so strong that day, the demon didn't stand a chance. It wasn't really the punch; it was the anointing when I touched her that made the demon go. Demons cannot stand being in an anointed service. They don't want to be around. They want to get out.

The Lady With The Cat

I remember during a week-long revival, there was a lady who came to our services every night. On the first night, she sat at the front. While I was preaching, she moved back six rows. She kept moving until she was at the back door. I was preaching and that lady was moving around because demons are restless. I saw her when she was at the back door, then I saw her try to leave. I signaled the pastor and an elder was sent to the lady, and she sat at the back. She did that for a couple of nights. One night she came up to me and handed me a piece of paper.

I had one more night of the revival, so I stuck the note in my pocket and took it with me to where I was staying. I was staying with the pastor and his wife. When I reached the house, I read the note to the pastor. It said, "I am a Satan worshiper and I belong to a Satanic church. The Satanic priest wants me to prove my alliance to him and to the church by killing my cat. So I have to kill my cat and bring my dead cat to the next meeting to prove to them that I will obey. But I don't want to kill my cat. I love my cat. It's just me alone with my cat, and I've had it for a long time. I don't want to kill my cat. I thought maybe I would try to come to a Christian church meeting, that maybe they would love me and let me keep my cat and I'd get out of the Satanic church."

We prayed and on the final night, she was there so I called her forward. She refused to come all the way up.

She came about halfway up so I went to her and talked to her. I didn't shout and scream for the demons to come out of her. I just hugged her and silently whispered in her ear, "Satan, you're going now." She was very quiet, as calm as one can be. I whispered in her ear with authority, and she slipped right out of my hands, went down on the floor and all the demons came out. When she got up, I asked her, "Are you ready to receive Jesus?"

She said, "I'm not sure."

I responded with the same question, "Would you like to accept Jesus right now?"

She said, "If I accept Jesus right now, the Satanic church is going to try to find me and kill me or hurt me or wound me or scar me because they do that. Will this church protect me if I accept Jesus?"

I was just a visitor passing through so I turned to the pastor and asked, "Will you guys make sure you take care of her?"

They said, "Actually, you can come live with us for a while so they can't find you."

They recognized the need for her to be discipled.

So she said, "You promise you'll let me stay with you for a while until I can relocate or so they can't find me?"

The pastor said, "We promise."

So she accepted Jesus as her Lord and Savior. The pastor and his wife were faithful to their word. They took her in and she stayed with them for six months and even helped her to relocate. Years later, I stopped by to visit a minister that I knew. When I went into the ministry center, I approached the secretary's desk to ask to see him and to my surprise, the secretary was none other but that lady. She gave me a quick update. She said, "After I left the Satanic church, I got to keep my cat. My cat did die a few years ago, but the pastor and his wife discipled me. I've been going to church and now I volunteer once a week to come in and help the ministry because it's just around the corner from where I live, and I donate my time for one day a week so the secretary can get a day off."

Do you see the importance of setting the captives free? There are people who are bound by demons that God has an appointed destiny for but Satan comes to abort and stop it. God wants us to know that we have the power to loose people who are bound and to set the captives free.

Bar Ministry

Sometimes we do witnessing in the local bars. One night I had some people I was teaching to do bar ministry. It was about midnight when suddenly one of the team members came for me and said, "Hurry, Sister Joan, they're trying to cast the devil out of somebody and I don't think they know how to do it."

So I ran to where they were. There were bars all around and there was a little corner where we set up our food station, etc, and they had a man there who was on the ground squirming. I stood over the man and said, "Satan, come out." He started to flip and growl like an animal and foaming at the mouth. All the bars started to empty out because they all wanted to see what was happening outside. A crowd started to gather in a circle watching me cast the devil out of the man. Finally, all the demons were cast out. I realized that I had an audience watching me because they had probably never seen anything like that. So, I said, "Don't be scared. This here is the power of God that has just set this man free."

I helped the man to his feet and said, "If you accept Jesus Christ as your Lord and Savior right now, the devil has no power over you anymore." Then I turned to the crowd and continued to say to the others, "If you want to ask Jesus in your heart, you can right now. Let's pray."

A few people prayed with me, including the man. I don't know if they meant the prayer or not, only God knows. Some of them did ask how they can be free as well and I told them that I would be preaching the next day at my church and I invited them to come. It was Saturday night. I had some cards with me with the name of the church and address, so I handed the cards to them and they went back into the bars.

At our local church, our pastor commissioned me to do a week-long Holy Ghost teaching. The day after our bar ministry outreach was the start of our week-long meeting at our church. When Marty and I pulled up to the church Sunday morning and got out of the car, some of the people from the bar were there. While walking towards the church, a lady came up to me and said, "I want to be set free like the guy last night on the street." So I started commanding the devil to come out. I didn't know she had a demon. I thought she was just being sarcastic. Suddenly, she was on the lawn and I was casting devils out of her and Marty was helping me. People started coming out of the church to watch me on the front lawn casting devils out.

My pastor sent one of the elders out. He came over to me while doing the deliverance and said, "Pastor says he wants you in the office right now."

I responded, "Tell pastor I'm busy."

I couldn't stop in the middle of the deliverance. I kept casting the devils out of the woman. The elder came out again and said, "Pastor's getting very upset with you. Stop what you're doing and come in."

I told him again, "I cannot stop what I'm doing. Tell him I'll be in when I get through."

Finally, the lady was set free and we lead her to the Lord. She was crying so I hugged her and said, "Come on in to the church service."

Marty turned to me and said, "You better go see what the pastor wants." He took her into the church and found her a seat while I went to the pastor's office.

My pastor was so upset. He said, "You know you're our speaker today so why are you out on the front lawn casting devils out of a lady, and how does that look? People walking by seeing that?"

I said, "But pastor, it doesn't matter how it looks. A lady needs to be set free. Jesus had demons show up in His services right in the middle of church service and He went ahead and set the people free."

He responded, "Yes, but you're our speaker. You have used up all the anointing on her and there's not going to be any anointing for our service."

There is no shortage of anointing. In fact, the more God uses you, the more you get anointed and the more God continues to use you, the stronger the anointing gets. We had a very powerful service that day.

Most Christians go to church every Sunday. If someone comes who needs to be set free, there should be ministers in the church who can pray for them to set them free or they will leave the same way they came. We need to set the captives free. We need to walk in that power and anointing and be ready at all times to be used powerfully by God.

Baby Christians Also Have Power

I was preaching at a church in Florida when a lady who came to the service came up for prayer. It was a Sunday night and when she came for prayer, I asked her if she wanted to accept Jesus as her Lord and Savior. She

181

started growling and manifesting a demon. So I took authority over that demon and commanded it to go. She fell to the floor, foaming at the mouth. They had to get her a bucket because she was vomiting. I kept commanding the devil to leave and I knew when all the demons were gone. I told the ushers to stand her up, so they helped her to her feet.

I said to her, "Now that those demons are gone, do you want to receive Jesus?"

She said, "Yes."

She accepted Jesus as her Lord and Savior and was then filled with the Baptism of the Holy Spirit. She was transformed.

She came back to church the next night because I was teaching people how to be a soul-winner. She was very hungry for the things of God. The next night, after the teaching service, we prayed for everyone there. After we dismissed, the baby Christian went to Denny's by herself. She felt the anointing so strongly, she didn't want to just go home and sleep. She was excited. So she was at Denny's and a waitress came over to her and was filling her coffee cup. The waitress said, "You sure are happy tonight. You come in quite often, but tonight you are just bubbling up and seem so happy."

The lady, who was only saved for two days, said, "Oh, yes because I got something last night." She started speaking in tongues and the waitress asked her what foreign language was she speaking. She said, "I don't know what it is. It's called the Baptism of the Holy Spirit. I don't understand all of it. I just started going to this church and all I know is when I do it, I feel really good and all my oppression is gone. It's better than any drugs I've ever taken in my life. I do it and I just feel so great."

The waitress said, "I really need what you have."

The new Christian lady asked, "What time do you get off?"

The waitress was off at eleven so the lady decided to wait for her.

When the waitress was off the clock for the night, they both went out to the lady's truck. The lady said, "First of all, you have to do what I did. I had to get saved and then you get the Baptism of the Holy Spirit. So repeat after me."

The waitress said, "No."

The lady repeated, "I said repeat after me."

The waitress continued to say, "No" repeatedly. So the lady said, "I know what is happening to you. That same thing happened to me. There's something holding you and hindering you." So the lady leans the waitress against the truck and said, "Come out, in the name of Jesus. I said come out in the name of Jesus." The waitress slithers down to the ground, leaning against the truck. Demons began to come out of her.

After the deliverance, the lady said to her, "Get up. Now you can get saved and you can get the Holy Spirit. That's how it happened to me. So that's how it's going to happen to you."

She led the waitress to the Lord and then led her to receive the Baptism of the Holy Spirit.

So, how soon can you cast out devils and set the captives free? Jesus said He has given us all power and authority. He also said we should not rejoice because we can cast out demons, but we should rejoice that our names are written in heaven.

When you are saved, your name is written in heaven. So, you have the authority and the power to lay hands on the sick and see them recover, speak in unknown tongues, raise the dead and cast out demons. Freely you have received, so freely you should give. Jesus said He has enabled us to do even greater works than what He did. You need to start moving in faith because there are many demonic oppressed men, women and children waiting for you to come and set them free by the power of Jesus Christ.

So, how long does it take for you to be used of God? The answer is immediately. God will use you as soon as you receive Jesus.

Conclusion

God has given you power and authority to go and set the captives free.

Then the seventy returned with joy, saying, "Lord, even the demons are subject to us in Your name." And He said to them, "I saw Satan fall like lightning from heaven. Behold, I give you the authority to trample on serpents and scorpions, and over all the power of the enemy, and nothing shall by any means hurt you. Nevertheless do not rejoice in this, that the spirits are subject to you, but rather rejoice because your names are written in heaven." (Luke 10:17-20).

How soon can you start doing deliverance? You were qualified from the very moment you said, "Dear Jesus, come into my heart and be my Lord and my Savior." You were given the keys to the kingdom; your name was written in heaven and you were empowered in that moment to go and set captives free.

If your name is written in heaven, you can do the works that God has called you to do.

> And He said to them, "Go into all the world and preach the gospel to every creature. He who believes and is baptized will be saved; but he who does not believe will be condemned. And these signs will follow those who believe: In My name they will cast out demons; they will speak with new tongues; they will take up serpents; and if they drink anything deadly, it will by no means hurt them; they will lay hands on the sick, and they will recover. (Mark 16:15-18).

Go preach the gospel with the power and the anointing of the Holy Spirit. Our prayer for you is that you will step out and set the captives free.

Mike's Testimony Of Hell

By Michael Yeager

My Journey To Hell Begins

One night I was deep in prayer with Willy, an African-American brother in my barracks. I had the privilege of seeing Willy come back to Christ. At one time, previously, he had walked with the Lord but had backslid. Before and after he was saved, our nickname for him was "Willy Wine" because now he was filled with new wine. As we were praying together, something very strange and very frightening began to happen to me. At the time of this event there was a gathering of some men in our battalion. They were having a party in the common area right outside our sleeping quarters where we were praying. The party they were having was quite loud with music and laughter, but it did not hinder us from crying out to God for souls.

As we were praying, I could sense that something was about to happen. The hair on the back of my arms and neck stood up on end. It was as if electricity was filling the very atmosphere around us. I sensed a strong tugging to go deeper in prayer. I gave myself completely over to the spirit of intercession, crying out to the Lord.

I began to cry out in prayer to God intensely, asking Him to allow me to have a supernatural experience of hell. I wanted this in order that I would have a greater and deeper compassion, a deeper love, a deeper understanding for the lost. I truly wanted to know the pains, the sorrows, the torments, the fears, and the agonies of those in hell. I wanted to weep and wail, to travail with a broken heart over the unconverted to reach them more effectively.

Please understand that I believe God put this desire, this prayer, into my heart for the love of souls. I began to pray in a realm that I had never been in before when suddenly an overwhelming and tangible darkness descended upon me.

"And when the sun was going down, a deep sleep fell upon Abram; and, lo, an horror of

great darkness fell upon him." (Genesis 15:12 -
KJV).

A frightening darkness enveloped me. Everything
around me disappeared. I no longer heard the music or
the party that was taking place. Even though Willy was
right there with me, I did not hear or see him. And it
seemed as if time itself had come to a stop. To my utter
shock, amazement, and horror, the floor and the
building around me began to shake more violently than
I had ever experienced before. Usually when we did get
a quake (Adak Alaska) it would only last a matter of
seconds. But in this situation the shaking did not stop
as it normally did, rather it increased.

The Floor Of The Building Ripped Open

All I could do at that moment was to try to hug the floor
and hang on for dear life. The darkness lifted, but I
could not see Willy anywhere. Then a terrible ripping
and grinding noise filled the air. I saw the floor of the
barracks ripple like that of a wave on the sea. The very
floor of the barracks that I was laying upon began to tear
and rip apart. I watched in stunned amazement and
horror as the floor tiles popped and stretched. The
concrete and steel within the building began to twist

and rip apart. And the floor I was laying on began to split and tear open right below me.

I immediately began to look for a way to get out of the building. Everything was shaking so violently that I could not get up off the floor to make a dash to escape. The dust and dirt in the room was so thick and heavy that I could hardly breathe. Now this rip in the floor began to enlarge and became an opening. I would call it more like a hole. I began to slip and fall into this hole; I tried desperately to reach for any kind of handhold that I could find. I began to scream and yell for help. But there was no one to help me. I became increasingly desperate trying to grab hold of something, anything that I could get my hands on. Objects around me began to fall through this hole in the floor. I watched as physical objects slipped past me into this hole and I could feel myself sliding more and more.

No matter how desperately I was trying to cling to and hold on to items to prevent my falling, there was nothing that I could do. Finally, I slipped and fell backward as if falling off a ladder. As I was falling, everything seemed to go into slow motion like film that is slowed for a preview. I was falling with parts of the crumbling building all around me. I watched as I fell past twisted steel beams, concrete floors, walls ripped into pieces, plumbing, and heating pipes, and sparking electric wires. I went past the underground tunnels that connected the buildings together.

The next thing I knew, I was falling past the ground and rock of the island. This terrible rip in the earth, this hole that I was falling down began to take on the form and similarity of that of a well, like an endless tube, an ever-proceeding pit. It became approximately three feet wide. As I was falling, I was desperately trying to grab hold of the rocks that were protruding from the sides of this deep dark pit, but my descent was too fast. None of the rocks seemed to protrude far enough for me to get a good handhold.

Even as I was falling down this hole, I was not experiencing any fear of going to hell or fear of dying because I had a calm assurance that I knew my heart was right with God. I was ready to meet my Savior. Don't misunderstand; I am not saying that I had no fear! Though I knew in my heart that I was right with God, I was still filled with the absolute horror of not knowing what was happening to me. At that moment I did not have any idea whatsoever that I was plunging into hell.

I kept trying to figure out how I could stop my descent into this hole. What I was experiencing was mind-boggling because, to me, it was truly, physically happening. I could feel, touch, smell, hear, and see everything that was happening to me. Actually, everything seemed to be amplified beyond my normal five senses. Through the years I had experienced dreams, nightmares, and hallucinations from drugs and alcohol which I had taken, but none of them came anywhere near to what I was experiencing at that very moment. My mind kept screaming, how can I stop my descent into this hole? I just kept on falling down and down into this really deep dark hole. Deeper and deeper I fell—down, down, down. I must have fallen mile after mile.

"He hath said, which heard the words of God, which saw the vision of the Almighty, falling into a trance, but having his eyes open." (Numbers 24:4 - KJV).

Terrible Stink Of Hell

Now as I was falling down this deep dark hole, a violent and overwhelming hot wind began blowing from somewhere at the bottom of this shaft hitting me in the face. It was a suffocating, nauseating, stinking wind. It smelled of rotting eggs and sulfur. It became almost impossible for me to breathe. I tried to use my shirt as a mask to filter out the stinking smell. But it was to no avail.

> **"Their slain also shall be cast out, and their stink shall come up out of their carcases, and the mountains shall be melted with their blood." (Isaiah 34:3 - KJV).**

Actually this experience in and of itself should have been enough to kill me. I kept trying to get a breath of fresh air, but there was none to be had. As I was desperately trying to breathe, I continued to fall. How long I fell down this hole I do not know. But it seemed to me to have no end, to be bottomless. Or was it? As I looked down in the direction that I was falling feet first, I looked between my feet. I began to see a very small and very faint orange, yellowish, reddish glow. It began extremely small, but as I continued to fall toward the light it became brighter and brighter.

Never-Ending Cavern Of Hell

Before I knew it, I was out of this black hole, this tunnel. I had entered into a humongous and gigantic, seemingly never-ending cavern. I could see no end in sight. It was as if I had fallen into a whole different world, an underworld. I was falling like a skydiver. Now, I was tens of thousands of feet above an ocean of liquefied, swirling lava and blazing fire.

Thousands of feet below me was a frightening, boiling lake of fire. It was burning, churning, and bubbling, almost similar to that of a pan of overheated boiling molasses on a stove. I could see that it was extremely aggravated and violent. It was almost as if it was filled and possessed with an aggressive, living fury. Fire and brimstone were exploding upon its surface in every direction sending flames rising thousands of feet into the air.

The flames darted here and there like a huge blazing gasoline fire. It would appear one moment in one area, vanish, and then appear somewhere else. At the same time there were air-shattering explosions, like volcanoes erupting across this vast surface of liquefied lava. It was like a living, swirling, obsessed whirlpool of fire, brimstone, and lava. It glowed different colors of red, orange, and yellow.

Perhaps a better description would be that it pulsated and radiated like hot charcoal in a furnace, with molten steel, liquefied stone, and swirling gases. Fire danced across the top of its surface like miniature tornadoes spinning violently out of control. They would spin until they ascended up into the black nothingness of the cavern into which I was falling.

Intense Heat In Hell

I continued to descend toward the surface of this ocean, this endless lake of liquid fire and lava, it seemed to me that I was about ten thousand feet above the surface of this ocean. And even at ten thousand feet, the heat that was hitting me was so intense that my very flesh felt as if it was withering, melting, and burning. It felt as if it was being ripped off of my hands, my face, and my body. In the past I have received minor burns from cooking or from building a fire to keep the house warm. But that was minor—a mosquito bite, compared to what was happening to me now.

As I looked at my skin and flesh, it was beginning to bubble and blister. My whole body was beginning to burn. My clothes were catching on fire, and I could not put them out. My shoes were melting to my feet. My hair caught on fire like the wick on a candlestick. It was as if someone had doused me with gasoline and then threw a match on me. I began to scream like a madman.

How could anyone truly experience what I am sharing with you and yet not be shaken to the very core of their being every time they retell their story? I'm telling you that as I recount to you what transpired, my heart is filled with dread and trembling. At that same time my lungs felt like they were going to be burned out of my chest. I needed cool fresh air, but there was none to be had. Can you imagine what it would be like to be roasted alive slowly over an open burning pit with red hot coals? This is what I was experiencing.

Dreadful Screams Of Hell

In the midst of this overwhelming pain and agony, my ears began to be filled with a strange, eerie sound—a humming sound, like a throbbing deep moan that never stopped. As I was falling closer and closer to the surface of the burning lava, this humming, groaning, moaning sound increased in intensity. It became an ear-piercing, overwhelming, never-ending sound that grew louder and louder. It was as if my head was surrounded by a huge hive of angry bees. As I continued to fall toward this churning, massive ocean, the sound that I was hearing became more distinct and clear. It contained ear-piercing highs and incredible heartbreaking lows with many other pitches in between that are too numerous to describe to you.

I remember asking myself in my pain and torment, "What in the world can this sound be that I am hearing? What could be causing such terrible heart wrenching, horror-filled sounds?" And then at that very moment, I believe that the Spirit of the Lord opened up my understanding to what was happening to me. It hit me like an eighteen-wheel truck slamming into my body.

The sound that I was hearing was not coming from equipment, machinery or something from nature. But it was coming from human beings, my friend. The sound that was coming to my ears was from human beings who were screaming, wailing, groaning, and moaning with an incredible, intense, overwhelming pain. They were in unbelievable agony with unbearable torments. My ears were filled with the terrible screams of damned souls.

"Therefore I will wail and howl, I will go stripped and naked." (Micah 1:8a - KJV).

**"And shall cast them into a furnace of fire: there shall be wailing and gnashing of teeth."
(Matthew 13:42 - KJV).**

I remember my whole body began to shake violently almost as if I were having convulsions. It was like rivers of absolute dismay and complete horror. The bitter lamentations of suffering humanity engulfed me. Oh how their sorrows flooded my very being. Even as I retell this story to you, it is as if my heart is being ripped out of my chest. And the agony and pain that I am experiencing right now is nothing compared to the agony that God is experiencing. You see, it is His will that none should perish. But all should have eternal life.

Like Bobbing Corks In Hell

At about two thousand feet above the surface of the ocean of hell, the pain that was hitting my body was overwhelming, unbearable, unbelievable, and all consuming. My lungs were on fire. My eyes felt like they were being burned out of my sockets. My clothes had burned and melted to my flesh. I was beyond third-degree burns.

And yet, incredibly, I was still fully aware of everything that was transpiring around me. If anything, my five senses were more alive than ever before. I believe that God must have supernaturally increased my capacity to experience all that I was going through.

I was looking down in the direction in which I was headed. I could see upon the surface of the lake of fire what looked like little black objects violently bobbing up and down like fishing corks in the orange and red glow of the burning, churning, bubbling ocean of hell. As my eyes became more focused (by the grace of God), I could see thousands upon tens of thousands of these objects dotting the surface. They were everywhere. As I looked upon them, I found myself possessed by an overwhelming curiosity. I lost interest in everything else that was happening to me.

Even though I was experiencing tremendous and unbelievable pain and agony, I was still able to focus my mind and attention upon these objects. My mind was very clear and sharp. The only way to describe my curiosity was that it was supernatural. This curiosity gripped my mind and heart. And as I fell closer and closer, I could see that these objects were actually oblong, not round as I had thought. But they contained limbs at both ends. And these limbs were waving back and forth, back and forth, in a frantic jerking type of motion.

Out of my innermost being, I let out a deep, tormented groan as I suddenly realized what I was looking at. These black, bobbing objects were nothing less than human beings! People! They were masses of humanity from every nation, culture, tribe, and tongue. And they were screaming, moaning, and yelling as they were being turned and tossed about, head over heels, carried along in the swirling lava of the burning, churning, undercurrents of hell.

Now, in my past I have heard people weeping and wailing, crying over the death of a precious loved one. I have experienced this myself when our four-and-a- half-year-old little girl, Naomi, died. That same year my mother died. I wailed and wept and cried. But never had I heard crying like this, such agony, such screaming, such sorrow.

The wailing and howls of pain broke my heart. It still breaks my heart to this day as I think upon this experience. I could not tell by looking upon these burning blackened masses of humanity who or what they were. It was only by the Spirit of God that I discern these truths. For when their physical body hit the flaming fires of hell, they lost their sexuality. They lost their nationality, their race and color of skin. No longer could you determine what their age was. For hell makes all people equal.

Dreadful Screams Of Hell

These are souls forever damned. These are souls with no hope, escape, help, or relief from pain. Maybe these are people you and I have known—dads and moms, brothers and sisters, aunts and uncles, neighbors and friends who have died without loving Christ. Their hearts were full of the cares and lusts of this world. Their lives were full of selfishness and sin. They had no time for God or His Word. They spent their lives pursuing the useless pleasures of this world, filling their minds with vain and useless amusements, foolish entertainment, ungodly movies, involving themselves in immoral activities. The Apostle Paul warned us:

"This know also, that in the last days perilous times shall come." (2 Timothy 3:1 - KJV).

Because God is a righteous God, He must judge sin. By the time these people discovered this truth, it was too late. For they died and woke up in a dreadful, boiling

203

lake of brimstone, sulfur, and fire. They have no way of escape, no relief from pain, and no hope for the future. These people have nothing to look forward to except endless torment, loneliness, and pain. Their bodies were burned black like burnt chicken that had been overcooked on a barbecue pit. The unquenchable flames of a never-ending hell blackened their souls. Those down there looked like living and moving pieces of charcoal.

Into the Lava Of Hell

Because I was so caught-up in the stark reality of what was going on before me, I did not realize that I was still falling closer and closer to the surface of the lake of fire. Suddenly, I plunged into the lava. It was like burning mud and quicksand. Immediately it sucked me in with a frightening ferocity. It engulfed me, pulling me down, swallowing me up in its hideous stomach of endless suffering and pain.

It covered me over and filled my mouth and my nose, ears and my eyes with an overwhelming, intense burning pain. The flaming sulfur of hell came into my mouth. It went down my throat, into my stomach, and filled my lungs. I was immersed in a baptism of absolute horror. My eyes felt like they were being consumed out of my sockets. And yet they were still there. My whole body was on fire and burning like a marshmallow dropped into the red coals of a campfire.

I came to the absolute bleak truth that in no way could hell ever be exaggerated. Everything I had ever heard or read about the eternal destiny of the lost and the damned, those who do not love God, does not sufficiently describe what I was experiencing right at that moment. No words could exist to describe the intense pain, the heart wrenching sorrow, the absolute agony, and the everlasting torments of hell. Hell is totally deaf to the cries and agonies of those who are swallowed up and wallowing in its belly.

"And death and hell were cast into the lake of fire. This is the second death. And whosoever was not found written in the book of life was cast into the lake of fire." (Revelation 20:14-15 - KJV).

Swallowed Up In The Darkness Of Hell

Now at that very moment excruciating pain overtook me. It penetrated my mind, and inflamed every fiber of my being. It stuck to my flesh like melted black tar. The lava was like burning mud that sucked me into the very depths of hell. Deeper and deeper I sunk. It pulled me down like a whirlpool. I wish I could be more graphic in how it felt. How deep I sunk I do not know. The depths of the oceans of this present world are nothing in comparison with the depths of hell. For it is called the bottomless pit. I could not resist its current. It pulled and sucked at me like quicksand. I gave up all hope of ever coming to the surface. I was covered and engulfed in total darkness. I could not see anything. Now you understand that my eyes were not burned out of my head. I could still see. And yet I could not see, because there was no light.

The Bible declares that there is no light in hell to be had. There is no light of the sun, the moon, the stars or even a flame. It is the darkness of eternal midnight. When I began this journey, and throughout it, for the most part I could see what was taking place. God allowed me to see because He wanted me to behold what was happening in the underworld of the lost. Those who are eternally lost in hell will never see light again because they have rejected the light of Jesus Christ. They will never have the privilege of seeing the glorious lights of creation again.

"But the children of the kingdom shall be cast out into utter darkness: there shall be weeping and gnashing of teeth." (Matthew 8:12 - KJV).

Cannot Die In Hell

Now, as I was sucked deeper into the lava, brimstone and sulfur, the burning mud of hell was in my mouth, and I could not breathe. My lungs were collapsing. I kept trying to suck in oxygen, but I could not. I was suffocating, and yet, I did not die. My flesh was burning, and yet, I did not die. My brain was being ripped apart from the pain and sensations in my body, and yet, I did not die. The flames of hell were burning my eyes, my tongue, my hands, and my belly from the crown of my head to the soles of my feet; I was in excruciating pain. The burning, boiling, searing, brimstone and sulfur of hell were penetrating every fiber of my being, and yet, I did not die. I am not in the least exaggerating my experience, if anything I am under-rating it.

As I was going through these terrible sensations, I felt an upward thrust pushing me toward the top of the lake of fire. A strong type of current was dragging me along. And then I came to the surface. I began bobbing up and down as I was being moved along, turning, end over end, head over heels, rolling and tumbling with the swirling masses of those around me in the violent waves and currents of hell. By now, you would think that all of my feelings would have been gone, burned out into nonexistence, that all of my five senses would have been seared into nothingness. You would think that I would have gone into absolute and total shock, that I would have been virtually and completely numb. But that was not the case, every one of my five senses was still very much alive.

I could touch, taste, hear, smell; I could see the torments of hell. Now I can tell you, my friend, by personal experience that the most extreme and bizarre torments that a person could ever experience on Earth is nothing compared to the never-ending torments of hell.

Eternity In Hell

There seemed to be no end to this nightmare called hell. A second dragged into an hour. A minute turned into a year, and an hour became an everlasting eternity. This was just the beginning of forever. There is no end to this place called hell. There is no escape. There is no exit. There is no way out. Hell is eternal; it is forever.

No Love In Hell

If you can imagine in the midst of the pain and agony, another even much greater and terrifying torment began to flood my soul. It was emotional, spiritual, psychological, and mental. Here in this place, this bubbling, boiling slime pit called hell, there is absolutely no love. It is totally void of all love. Even when I was a sinner, I was surrounded by the love of God; His goodness, provision, and blessings. I may not have recognized or even realized it. Whether I knew it or not, God was watching over me. He was protecting, helping, and reaching out to me, even though I was not serving Him or loving Him.

All Alone In Hell

A loneliness and emptiness beyond description descended upon me. Even though I bumped into many others, there was no communication. You have no recognition of friends and relatives. Those in hell are tormented devils and souls. They are filled with dreadful shrieks, screams caused by the fierceness of their pains. There are fearful blasphemies against God's power and justice who keeps them there. The torments of fellow sufferers do nothing to relieve you of your miseries. It only increases them. And every soul that you lead into hell with you will only magnify your sorrows a hundredfold. Dad and mom, pastor and preacher, teacher and politician, can you live with yourself knowing you are taking some you love to hell with you?

Endless Pain In Hell

In hell there is no relief, no freedom from pain. One's body does not go numb; rather, the pain intensifies. Every part of the soul, body, mind, emotions, and our total being is tormented at once. The human body is a wonderful and marvelous creation.

"I will praise thee; for I am fearfully and wonderfully made: marvelous are thy works; and that my soul knoweth right well." (Psalm 139:14 - KJV).

And yet, amazingly, the soul of man also has a body. The natural eye cannot see the body of the soul, but that does not mean it does not exist. Your soul in this life looks exactly like your physical body. But in heaven, if you die in Christ, you will receive a glorified body, a body that is glorious and amazing. The unrepentant sinner will be cast into the lake of fire with the devil and his angels. (See John 5:28-29, 1 Thessalonians 4:16, and Daniel 12:2).

God must put an end to the sinful shenanigans of the Satanic nature. The pain, suffering, agony, and torment of eternal damnation restrain and hinder the Satanic nature, but it cannot cleanse the human heart, soul, mind, will, and emotions from the seed of sin. Only through the sacrificial work of Jesus Christ and loving Him can our hearts be cleansed from this dreadful seed of sin.

How long I had been in hell, I do not know. It seemed like an eternity. I had been crying out in pain and agony unconsciously, screaming and wailing like the rest of the damned. And yet my cries were of a totally different nature. Their cries were cursing, profanity, wickedness, begging, and promises of repentance if given another chance. Curses were only to be followed by more curses. The realm of hell is filled with the noise of the damned, weeping and wailing and crying. They were shouting and screaming and yelling and moaning in terrible overwhelming pain. And yet those who are in hell now understand their spiritual condition and that their punishment is just and proper. They understand that they alone are to blame for their present situation and eternal damnation.

Now my cries were to God, justifying, praising, worshiping, and acknowledging that from God came my help. I remember screaming in pain that God is righteous in His judgments and that He is true and faithful and worthy of all glory and honor. From my heart and soul, out of my mouth came a nonstop flow of love and devotion, praise and worship to the Three in One. It might be hard to believe that someone filled with such overwhelming pain and agony could be worshiping and praising God, and yet that's what I was doing. The Scriptures declare for out of the abundance of the heart the mouth speaks. Then, from somewhere within I cried out for deliverance.

"Though he slay me, yet will I trust in him: but I will maintain mine own ways before him." (Job 13:15 - KJV).

"A good man out of the good treasure of his heart bringeth forth that which is good; and an evil man out of the evil treasure of his heart bringeth forth that which is evil: for of the abundance of the heart his mouth speaketh. And why call ye me, Lord, Lord, and

do not the things which I say?" (Luke 6:45-46 - KJV).

God Heard Me In Hell

In the midst of my prayers, I heard a voice that seemed to come from heaven. It was a majestic, thunderous and awesome sound. This voice completely overwhelmed all of the sensations I was experiencing at that moment. It literally grabbed hold of me and placed me in a protective bubble. All of my blistered and burning flesh was instantly healed and made whole. My hair, clothes, and body were returned to their original condition just as they were before my journey began. The love and goodness of God came rushing back into my heart and mind.

The sorrows and woes of hell disappeared. This voice had an amazing effect upon hell. It shook the very foundations of the lake of fire itself. I heard the audible voice of God say, "Let My servant go." The bowels of hell twisted and turned as if in torment. They ripped apart like the Red Sea must have when Moses stretched forth his rod. Hell had no choice but to obey the voice of the Lord of heaven, earth, and hell.

"And said, I cried by reason of my affliction unto the LORD, and he heard me; out of the belly of hell cried I, and thou heardest my voice" (Jonah 2:2 - KJV).

"The sorrows of hell compassed me about; the snares of death prevented me; In my distress I called upon the LORD, and cried to my God: and he did hear my voice out of his temple, and my cry did enter into his ears. Then the earth shook and trembled; the foundations of heaven moved and shook, because he was wroth. There went up a smoke out of his nostrils, and fire out of his mouth devoured: coals were kindled by it. He bowed the heavens also, and came down; and darkness was under his feet." (2 Samuel 22:6-10 - KJV).

Out Of Hell

At that very moment, it was almost like hell itself vomited me out. Incredibly, it felt like I was being shot out of a canon.

NOTE: You can order books by Michael Yeager on Amazon.com.

Things That Open Doors To Demons

Ouija Board	Psychic Hotline
Palm Reading	Voodoo
Automatic Writing	Freemasonry
ESP/Mind Control	Superstition
Hypnotism	Spirit Guides
Horoscope	Animal Totems
Astrology	Witchcraft
Fortune Telling	Satanism
Water Witching	Numerology
Tarot Cards	Curandero
Pendulum	Satanic Music: *Hard*
Incantations	*Rock, Heavy Metal, etc.*
Charms of Protection	Reflexology
Crystals	Magnetic Healing
Crystal Balls	Iridology
False Religions	Yoga (any form)
Tai-Chi	Twilight Series
Reiki	Vampirism
Feng shui	

Martial Arts	Witchcraft Movies, Video
Acupuncture	and Board Games,
Transcendental	Cartoons and Books
Meditation	Biofeedback Mach.
Energy Healing	Chain Letters
Seances	Dream Catchers
Table/Body Lifting	Medicine Wheels
Reincarnation	Mediums
Dungeons & Dragons	Witchcraft, Wicca
Channeling	Good Luck Charms
Obeah, Santeria	Rabbit's Foot
Psychic Healing	Halloween
Applied Kinesiology	Sexual Sins
Biofeedback	Prescription Drug Abuse
	Alcohol

Keys To Soul Winning

I.   Questions to Ask

1. If you were to die right now, do you know for sure that you would go to Heaven?

2. Suppose you died and were standing before God. If He asked you why He should let you into Heaven, what would you say?

3. Could I take a moment to share with you, so that you can be sure what would happen if you were to die?

II.   Salvation

1. Every person must be born again to know God and have everlasting life (John 3:3; John 3: 16).

2. The reason why we must be born again is found in Romans 3:23 (all have sinned).

3. Romans 6:23 - For the wages of sin is death, but the gift of God is eternal life in Christ Jesus our Lord.

4. Being saved or born again is receiving Jesus as your Lord (Master) and committing yourself to follow His Word (Romans 10:9-10).

5. Ask the person if they believe that Jesus died for them and that God raised Jesus from the dead. If they believe these two things, they can be saved.

6. Ask to take the person's hand. Bow your head in prayer. YOU pray. Ask them to pray with you. (They repeat a phrase-by-phrase prayer after you.)

7. Pray this prayer with them: *"Jesus, I ask You to come into my life. I confess with my mouth that Jesus is my Lord. I believe in my heart that God has raised Jesus from the dead. I turn my back on sin. I repent of all my sins. I am now a child of God. Thank you Jesus for saving me."*

8. Tell them to tell someone else about their salvation experience. "Now tell someone today that you received Jesus as your Savior."

III. Follow Through

1. "You are now born again, forgiven and on your way to Heaven." Show them that they are now

the "righteousness of God" in Christ (2 Corinthians 5:17-21). Also, share about their need to renew their minds (Romans 12:1-2).

2. Invite them to come to church and start discipling them.

Steps To Baptism In The Holy Spirit

1. **The Holy Spirit is the source of a powerful life.**

a. **Acts 1:8.** "Power" and abundant strength and ability to be an overcomer and live a victorious life.

b. **John 14:26.** Comforter and teacher, who helps you in your everyday life situations.

c. **Acts 19:1-2,5-6.** Baptism of the Holy Spirit is a separate experience from the work of the Holy Spirit in conversion.

d. **Acts 10:44-46.** People were filled with the Holy Spirit and spoke in tongues.

2. **What happens when you are filled with the Holy Spirit?**

Acts 2:4

And they were all filled with the Holy Spirit and began to speak with other tongues, as the Spirit gave them utterance.

The Holy Spirit is already here for every born again person. You do not need to wait for Him. Just ask to receive the Holy Spirit.

Acts 2:38-39

Then Peter said to them, "Repent, and let every one of you be baptized in the name of Jesus Christ for the remission of sins; and you shall receive the gift of the Holy Spirit. "For the promise is to you and to your children, and to all who are afar off, as many as the Lord our God will call."

3. **Your mind won't understand or gain anything from speaking in tongues.** (It will sound useless and foolish). You are speaking mysteries to God, not to man.

1 Corinthians 14:2

For he who speaks in a tongue does not speak to men but to God, for no one understands him; however, in the spirit he speaks mysteries.

1 Corinthians 14:14-15

For if I pray in a tongue, my spirit prays, but my understanding is unfruitful. What is the conclusion then? I will pray with the spirit, and I will also pray with the understanding. I will sing with the spirit, and I will also sing with the understanding.

Speaking in tongues is an act of your will. God will not force you to do it, or do it for you.

4. **If you ask for the Holy Spirit in faith, you will receive Him.**

Luke 11:13

"If you then, being evil, know how to give good gifts to your children, how much more will your Heavenly Father give the Holy Spirit to those who seek Him."

5. **Have the person ask for the Holy Spirit (Luke 11:13).** Then lead them into a prayer inviting the Holy Spirit to fill them.
6. **Pray for them.** Let them know that they, as an act of faith, must open their mouth and let the Holy Spirit fill them.

7. **Have them pray this prayer:** "*Father*, I am asking you for the gift of the Holy Spirit. *Jesus*, baptize me with the Holy Spirit and fire. *Dear Holy Spirit*, come into me and fill me."

About Channel Of Love Ministries

Evangelist Joan Pearce was radically saved in 1977, and shortly afterward moved to Washington State. There she was greatly inspired and discipled by the daughter and son-in-law of the late Evangelist John G. Lake. God asked Joan to step out and do a home Bible study, even though she couldn't read.

Joan recognized God's hand was on her, and that He was calling her into ministry. Her heart cry is for souls and to fulfill Luke 4:18-19, to preach the Gospel to the poor, heal the brokenhearted, and bring healing and freedom to the hurting and oppressed – "to proclaim the acceptable year of the Lord."

Today, Joan continues in fulltime ministry, traveling across the United States and overseas. Channel of Love Ministries is doing "God is Taking the City" campaigns, where Joan and her husband, Marty, are seeing churches come together in unity to evangelize their cities. Joan also does revivals, church meetings, and citywide crusades where thousands come to Jesus. Part of her ministry is to teach practical evangelism classes and to conduct Holy Spirit Miracle Services where there are many notable and creative miracles. She and Marty have a heart to feed and clothe the needy and have ministered to the poor throughout the world.

Joan is on TV across the United States and is on the internet worldwide. The Channel of Love Ministries website is **www.joanpearce.org**. She and Marty are fulfilling God's great commission to "Go into all the world and preach the gospel" (Mark 16:15.)

Additional Books By Joan Pearce

Helping you to grow spiritually and share your faith more effectively!

Jesus, He is Your Answer

Price $5.00

This book is perfect for those who have just asked Jesus into their hearts. You may not know where to go from there.

This book will cover the experience you have had and outline the next few steps of your journey in establishing your Christian life through faith practices and principles that will solidify your foundation in Jesus Christ.

JOAN PEARCE

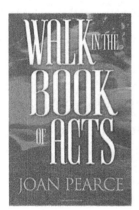

Faith Builders

Price $15.00

Your answer to life and victory. Yes, victory in your life comes through ONE way, Jesus Christ and Him crucified, God's only begotten Son. Here is the answer you have been looking for. Are you ready for the answer?

Walk in the Book of Acts

Price $18.00

Get ready to go to the next level. Jesus told his disciples, "Greater things will you do because I'm going to my Father." He then instructed them. 'Wait until you are filled with the Holy Spirit' This book will catapult you to the next level so you too can walk, live and see miracles just as Jesus did.

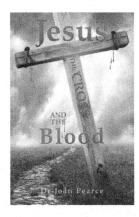

Jesus, the Cross and the Blood
Price $18.00

JESUS, THE CROSS, AND THE BLOOD will prepare you to be ready for what is coming very soon to planet earth. This book is about Jesus' journey to the Cross, and explains all the times He shed His precious blood on His way to Calvary, and how each of those moments affect our lives today.

By His Stripes, You Are Healed
Price $18.00

Do you want to see notable miracles? This book will equip you with the keys and knowledge to experience the miraculous for yourself and others.

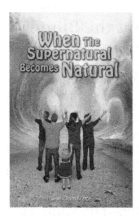

When The Supernatural Becomes Natural

Price $15.00

Hearing God and responding to His voice is crucial for every believer – especially today!

Yes, YOU Can Hear GOD Too!

Price $15.00

Every believer has the right to hear from Heaven. This down to earth book will challenge you to hear from God!

Let's Go Fishing!

Price $15.00

Are you wondering: "What is God's purpose and plan for my life? How do you draw your loved ones and others to the Lord? How can you help your church or group reach out to the lost and needy?" This book answers your questions.

Now's the Time Bible Studies

Price $10.00

Here are precious keys for unlocking and releasing God-given provision, power and authority into your life, and experiencing the precious love of Jesus. You'll grow spiritually – and be able to share what you've learned with others.

The Empty Spot

Price per pkg. of 10 $12.00

An excellent booklet for getting people saved and for discipling those who have recently received Jesus. This book has led thousands to Jesus. It's a great witnessing tool!

The Holy Spirit And Power

Price $15.00

One of the most profound mysteries in the scriptures is the Holy Spirit and His Power. Evangelist Joan unwraps some of these mysteries and clears up some confusion on this topic in the powerful book. The unsaved as well as the Church need to see a real demonstration of the Holy Spirit today and this book will help empower you for it.

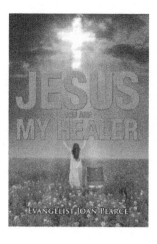

Jesus – You Are My Healer
Price $18.00

Have you ever asked yourself why some people are healed and others are not? Would you like to know what hindrances are blocking yours and others' healing? This book will answer help you answer some of these questions.

Are you ready to receive your healing? Then let's go...

Contacting Channel Of Love Ministries

Visit: www.joanpearce.org

- ✓ To write us a note, praise report or prayer request
- ✓ To see our TV show, *"Now is the Time for Miracles."*
- ✓ Learn more about our ministry and its goals
- ✓ Receive more details about "God is Taking the City" campaigns
- ✓ Offer financial and practical support
- ✓ See our current schedule
- ✓ Come to our Schools of Ministry
- ✓ Learn about opportunities to participate in Channel of Love Ministries' trips
- ✓ Get information on scheduling meetings for your church or group
- ✓ Order books, CD's and DVD's
- ✓ Sign up for our free Newsletter
- ✓ Download our free ministry helps
  and much more

We look forward to hearing from you!

Made in the USA
Monee, IL
28 January 2020